Dining In

with SHOW ME St. LOUIS

11 years of memorable recipes

NEWSCHANNEL 5
H a place to call
ome

SHOW ME St.LOUIS

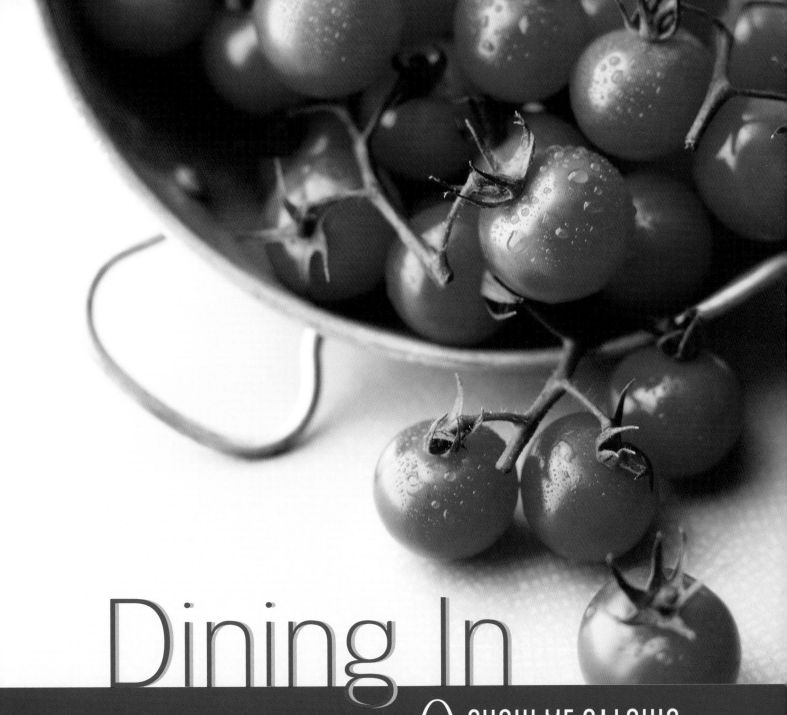

Dining In

with ⬯ SHOW ME St. LOUIS

11 years of memorable recipes

Dining In

with SHOW ME St. LOUIS

11 years of memorable recipes

Published by KSDK-TV

Copyright © 2007 by
KSDK-TV
1000 Market St.
St. Louis, Missouri 63101
314-421-5055

Cover Design: Kristin Fesler
Cover Photo: © www.veer.com
Chapter Opener Photographs © by: Barbara Newman
Front Matter Images: KSDK stock video
Special Thanks To: Liz Crider and Stephanie Zoller

This cookbook is a collection of favorite recipes,
which are not necessarily original recipes.

Library of Congress Control Number: 2006931741
ISBN-10: 0-9788250-0-4
ISBN-13: 978-0-9788250-0-3

Edited, Designed, and Manufactured by
Favorite Recipes® Press
An imprint of

FRP™

P. O. Box 305142
Nashville, Tennessee 37230
800-358-0560

Art Director: Steve Newman
Book Design: Starletta Polster
Project Manager: Cathy Ropp
Project Editor: Jane Hinshaw

Manufactured in China
First Printing: 2007
10,000 copies

Contents

NEWSCHANNEL 5

a place to call Home

Dear Friend,

Thank you for buying this cookbook! Not only have you purchased a unique book with delicious recipes featured on KSDK's "Show Me St. Louis," you are also helping find homes for children. Every day in greater St. Louis, three children are removed from their birth families because of abuse, abandonment, or neglect and must enter foster care. Today, more than four thousand children are in care and five hundred of these are waiting for a family to adopt them.

KSDK is proud of its strong commitment to the St. Louis community. We have a long history and are privileged to support some amazing community projects like the Komen St. Louis Race for the Cure, MDA Telethon, and "A Place to Call Home."

In 2002, KSDK partnered with the Foster & Adoptive Care Coalition for an adoption project called "A Place to Call Home." This segment was created to find adoptive families for some of the hardest children to place — older children and sibling groups. Each week our station features a child in foster care participating in a fun activity that allows his or her personality to shine.

"A Place to Call Home" is an award-winning and successful program. Fifty percent of the featured children have been placed in adoptive homes. The program broadens community awareness about the critical need for caring, nurturing foster/adoptive homes and highlights a "little wish" of the child. The Little Wishes program was created to provide normal childhood experiences that foster families often can't afford, like a first bike, swimming or ballet lessons, or attending a Cardinals game.

At KSDK, we believe that every child needs and deserves a forever family to love them and help them to heal from the trauma they have endured. A portion of the proceeds from the purchase of this cookbook support the important work of the Foster & Adoptive Care Coalition to find loving, supportive homes for our children.

Thank you again for purchasing this cookbook and making a difference in the lives of children.

Warmest Regards,

Lynn Beall

Lynn Beall
President, General Manager KSDK

In September 1995, **Show Me St. Louis** was born. The program was launched with hosts Debbye Turner, John Pertzborn, and reporters Wendy Bell and Dan Buck. Over the years, the faces may have changed but the show continues to provide St. Louisans with thirty minutes of good news about our community every weekday.

Whether it's the Arch or the Science Center, Debbye Turner or Heidi Glaus, **Show Me St. Louis** has been your passport — your ticket — to the fun places to go and the interesting things to do in St. Louis.

And what would **Show Me St. Louis** be without food? Each and every week we take you inside some of St. Louis's best restaurants and share some of their most sought after recipes. You'll find many of those recipes in the pages of this book.

We here on the staff of **Show Me St. Louis** love our city, and we love showing you all the great things it has to offer. We hope you enjoy your new cookbook, and join us each weekday at 3 PM, as we bring you many more years of delicious recipes.

Appetizers

Gateway Arch

I feel happy when
I think of adoption
because I think it
will be good for me;
it will be a different
world. To me being
adopted means that
you will have a family
till you grow up.
I would like my family
to have respect for one
another. I would like
my family to have love.
My expectation of
a forever family is that
they will be there for me.

Chrystal, age 13, in foster care

Many children in foster care have to make new friends every time they move to a new home. For her Little Wish,
Chrystal asked to go to Build-A-Bear Workshop® so she could build a new friend to take everywhere. She spent hours in the
Build-A-Bear Workshop® thoughtfully picking out every little detail of her new friend. Dressed in a pink cheerleader outfit,
with running shoes to match, Chrystal's new friend "Princess" was ready to go anywhere and everywhere.

Taco Beef Nuggets with Tejano Dipping Sauce

THANKS TO THE MISSOURI BEEF COUNCIL

1	pound ground round
2	tablespoons taco seasoning mix
1	(4-ounce) can chopped mild green chiles, drained
16	($1/2$-inch) cubes Colby Jack cheese
1	egg white
1	tablespoon water
2	cups crushed nacho cheese-flavored tortilla chips
6	tablespoons thick taco sauce
3	tablespoons honey

Combine the ground round, taco seasoning mix and green chiles in a bowl and mix lightly. Divide the mixture into sixteen portions and shape each portion around a cheese cube, enclosing the cheese completely.

Beat the egg white with the water in a bowl. Place the crushed tortilla chips in a bowl. Dip each meatball into the egg white mixture and then into the chips, coating well. Press each meatball lightly into a nugget shape with the palm and recoat with the chips if necessary.

Place the nuggets in a baking pan sprayed with nonstick cooking spray; spray the tops of the nuggets. Bake at 400 degrees for 15 to 20 minutes or until the nuggets are no longer pink and the juices run clear, 160 degrees internally.

Combine the taco sauce and honey in a microwave-safe dish and microwave on High for 30 seconds or until warm. Serve with the nuggets.

Makes 16 nuggets

Savory Sausage
Hors d'Oeuvre

THANKS TO THE CLEVER CLEAVER BROTHERS

1	pound mild, sweet or hot Italian sausage
4	garlic cloves, minced
1/2	cup minced Georgia pecans
1/4	cup minced dried apricots
1/4	cup dried cranberries
1	tablespoon chopped cilantro
1/2	cup (2 ounces) grated Parmesan cheese
15	round crackers
1/4	cup (1 ounce) grated Parmesan cheese
15	Georgia pecan halves

Remove the sausage from the casings and crumble into a bowl, discarding the casings. Add the garlic, minced pecans, apricots, cranberries, cilantro and 1/2 cup Parmesan cheese; mix well.

Shape by heaping tablespoonfuls into fifteen patties 3 inches in diameter. Fry in a nonstick skillet over medium heat for 3 minutes on each side. Remove to a paper towel to drain.

Arrange the crackers on a serving plate and top each with a sausage patty. Sprinkle with 1/4 cup Parmesan cheese and top each with a pecan half. Serve warm.

The patties can be prepared in advance, wrapped tightly in plastic wrap and stored in the refrigerator or freezer until time to cook.

This recipe was tested with Johnsonville Italian sausage.

Makes 15

Dining In

The original host, Debbye Turner, was
Miss America in 1990.

Superbowl Rustica

THANKS TO HAUTLY CHEESE

1 loaf French bread
1 pound sweet Italian sausage, casings removed
1 small red bell pepper, seeded and chopped
2 garlic cloves, chopped
1 small onion, chopped
1 (10-ounce) package frozen spinach, thawed and squeezed dry
salt and pepper to taste
15 ounces Hautly part-skim ricotta cheese
1/2 cup (2 ounces) grated Hautly Parmesan cheese
1/2 roll pepperoni, chopped
2 cups (8 ounces) shredded Hautly mozzarella cheese
1 teaspoon oregano
1 teaspoon crushed red pepper flakes

Cut the French bread into halves and split the halves lengthwise. Hollow out the bread to make four shells, discarding the bread or reserving it for another use. Cook the sausage in a skillet over medium-high heat, stirring until brown and crumbly. Add the bell pepper, garlic and onion and sauté for 3 to 5 minutes. Stir in the spinach and remove from the heat. Season with salt and pepper. Combine with the ricotta cheese, Parmesan cheese and pepperoni in a large bowl and mix well. Spoon the mixture into the bread shells and sprinkle with the mozzarella cheese.

Place on a baking sheet and bake at 425 degrees for 10 minutes or until the cheese melts and the bread is crisp. Sprinkle with oregano and red pepper flakes.

Serves 8 to 12

Quick Barbecued Chicken Wings

2   pounds chicken wing drumettes
1/4 cup barbecue sauce
1/4 cup chili sauce
2   teaspoons red wine vinegar
1   tablespoon honey
1   tablespoon soy sauce
1/2 teaspoon dry mustard
1/8 teaspoon ground red pepper

Place the drumettes in a 10-inch nonstick skillet. Combine the barbecue sauce, chili sauce, vinegar, honey, soy sauce, dry mustard and red pepper in a bowl and mix well. Spoon over the chicken. Bring to a boil and reduce the heat. Cook, covered, over medium-low heat for 20 to 25 minutes or until cooked through, stirring occasionally.

Serves 6 to 8

Buffalo Horns

THANKS TO THE MISSOURI EGG COUNCIL

1/4 cup chopped cooked chicken
buffalo wing sauce
6   hard-cooked eggs,
    cut into halves
1/4 cup (1/2 stick) butter, softened
1   tablespoon sour cream
1   teaspoon chopped celery
1/2 teaspoon Tabasco sauce
5   teaspoons buffalo wing sauce
salt and pepper to taste
chopped celery for garnish

Combine the chicken with enough buffalo wing sauce to cover in a small bowl. Let stand for 5 minutes or longer.

Mash the egg yolks in a small bowl. Add the butter and sour cream and mix well. Add 1 teaspoon celery and the Tabasco sauce. Remove the chicken from the marinating sauce and discard the sauce. Add to the egg yolk mixture and stir in 5 teaspoons buffalo wing sauce. Season with salt and a generous amount of pepper.

Spoon the mixture into the egg whites and garnish with additional celery. Chill for 15 to 20 minutes to develop the flavors before serving.

Makes 12

Crab Cakes

THANKS TO SOULARD'S RESTAURANT

1/4 cup chopped green bell pepper
3 tablespoons olive oil
1/3 cup chopped onion
3/4 cup chopped green onions
1 tablespoon minced garlic
1 egg
5 tablespoons grated
    Parmesan cheese
1/4 cup seasoned bread crumbs
1 pound jumbo lump crab meat
2 eggs
1 cup 2% milk
2/3 cup all-purpose flour
1/2 teaspoon salt
1/2 teaspoon white pepper
freshly ground black pepper to taste
seasoned bread crumbs for coating
3 tablespoons olive oil
1 tablespoon grated
    Parmesan cheese
fresh parsley and lemon twists
    for garnish

Sauté the bell pepper in 3 tablespoons olive oil in a skillet for 1 minute. Add the onion, green onions and garlic and sauté until tender. Combine with 1 egg, 5 tablespoons Parmesan cheese and 1/4 cup bread crumbs in a bowl and mix well. Fold in the crab meat and shape into 2-ounce crab cakes.

Whisk 2 eggs with the milk in a bowl. Place the flour, salt, white pepper and black pepper in a bowl. Place additional seasoned bread crumbs in another bowl. Coat the crab cakes with the flour. Dip the crab cakes into the egg mixture and coat well with the bread crumbs.

Sauté the crab cakes in 3 tablespoons olive oil in a skillet until golden brown. Sprinkle with 1 tablespoon Parmesan cheese and garnish with fresh parsley and twists of lemon. You can also serve these over capellini with lemon butter sauce.

Serves 10

Supa Shrimp Bruschetta

THANKS TO THE CLEVER CLEAVER BROTHERS

2 tablespoons extra-virgin olive oil

4 garlic cloves, minced

1 pound (31- to 40-count) shrimp, peeled, deveined and tails removed

1 tablespoon dried oregano

1/4 teaspoon salt

1/8 teaspoon pepper

1 tablespoon hot sauce

1/4 cup balsamic vinegar

1 1/2 cups chopped Roma tomatoes

1/2 cup chopped sweet onion

1/2 cup pitted black Greek olives, cut into halves

1/2 cup chopped marinated artichoke hearts

1/4 cup fresh basil, cut into thin strips

12 slices rustic bread

Heat a sauté pan over medium-high heat and add the olive oil and garlic. Sauté for 30 seconds. Add the shrimp to the skillet and sprinkle with half the dried oregano. Sauté for 1 minute or until the shrimp begin to turn pink. Turn the shrimp over and sprinkle with the remaining dried oregano. Season with salt and pepper and sauté for 1 minute. Stir in the hot sauce and balsamic vinegar. Sauté for 30 seconds and remove from the heat.

Mix the tomatoes, onion, olives, artichoke hearts and fresh basil in a bowl. Add the shrimp mixture and mix well. Spoon onto the bread slices and enjoy the big game.

This recipe was tested with Colavita extra-virgin olive oil, Colavita balsamic vinegar and Cholula hot sauce.

Makes 10 to 12

The first story to air on *Show Me St. Louis* was about Six Flags.

Dining In

Chipotle Chile Bruschetta

1/2 cup mayonnaise
2 tablespoons tomato-garlic tapenade
2 chipotle chiles in adobo sauce, seeded and chopped
2 tablespoons adobo sauce
1 1/4 cups (5 ounces) shredded Monterey Jack cheese
1/2 teaspoon dried cilantro
1/2 cup sourdough bread crumbs
10 thick slices tomato basil bread

Combine the mayonnaise, tapenade, chipotle chiles, adobo sauce, Monterey Jack cheese, cilantro and bread crumbs in a medium bowl; mix well.

Cut the bread slices into rounds with a large round cutter. Arrange on a baking sheet and toast lightly in a 400-degree oven. Cool for 5 minutes. Spread 1 tablespoon of the chipotle mixture on each bread slice and bake for 10 minutes or until the topping begins to puff and melt. Cool slightly before serving.

This recipe was tested with Saint Louis Bread Co. bread.

Serves 8

Confetti Nibbles

THANKS TO THE MISSOURI EGG COUNCIL

20 small round red potatoes
1/2 cup reduced-fat ranch salad dressing
1 teaspoon onion salt
1 teaspoon dried dill weed, or 1 tablespoon chopped fresh dill weed
6 hard-cooked eggs, chopped
1/2 cup finely chopped green onions with tops
1/2 cup finely chopped red bell pepper
fresh dill sprigs for garnish

Combine the potatoes with enough water to cover in a large saucepan. Bring to a boil and reduce the heat. Simmer for 15 to 20 minutes or until the potatoes are tender. Drain and cool.

Cut each potato into halves and cut a small slice off the bottom of each so it will stand upright. Scoop out the center of each potato half carefully with a spoon, leaving firm shells. Chop the scooped-out centers, reserving the shells.

Combine the salad dressing, onion salt and dill weed in a medium bowl. Add the eggs, green onions, red bell pepper and chopped potato; mix well.

Spoon the egg mixture into the potato shells. Place on a serving plate and cover. Chill in the refrigerator to blend the flavors. Garnish with fresh dill sprigs.

Makes 40

Apple Cider and Cheddar Fondue

4   cups (16 ounces) shredded
    sharp Cheddar cheese
3 1/2 teaspoons cornstarch
1 1/4 cups sparkling apple cider
1/4 cup lemon juice
1/8 teaspoon ground cinnamon
1/8 teaspoon ground nutmeg
1/2 teaspoon salt
freshly ground pepper to taste

Toss the Cheddar cheese and cornstarch in a medium bowl. Combine the apple cider and lemon juice in a medium saucepan with a heavy bottom. Bring just to a simmer over medium heat. Add the cheese mixture gradually, stirring until the cheese melts after each addition. Stir in the cinnamon, nutmeg, salt and pepper. Cook over low heat for 3 to 5 minutes or until thickened.

Spoon the mixture into an enamel or ceramic fondue pot and keep warm over a fondue burner. Serve immediately with chicken, pork sausages, waffle pieces, pizzelles, strudel, apple wedges or Cheddar cheese cubes.

Serves 10

Artichoke and Feta Dip

1   (14-ounce) can artichoke
    hearts, drained
1   (2-ounce) jar chopped pimento
8   ounces feta cheese, crumbled
2   tablespoons grated
    Parmesan cheese
2   tablespoons bread crumbs
1   garlic clove, minced
1/2 teaspoon crushed dried
    basil leaves
2/3 cup mayonnaise
3/4 teaspoon salt
1/8 teaspoon cayenne pepper

Reserve 3 artichoke leaves and several pieces of pimento for garnish. Chop the remaining artichoke hearts. Combine the feta cheese, Parmesan cheese, bread crumbs, garlic, basil, mayonnaise, salt and cayenne pepper with the remaining artichoke hearts and pimento in a lightly greased 1-quart baking dish.

Bake at 350 degrees for 25 to 30 minutes or until heated through. Garnish with the reserved artichoke leaves and pimento. Serve with pita chips, breadsticks, crackers and/or French bread.

Makes 2 1/2 to 3 cups

Appetizers

White Bean Mash

THANKS TO THE KELLY TWINS

2 (15-ounce) cans cannelloni
beans, cooked and drained
2 Roma tomatoes, seeded and
chopped (optional)
2 tablespoons finely chopped
Italian parsley
2 teaspoons minced garlic
1/4 cup extra-virgin olive oil
juice of 1 lemon
1 teaspoon ground cumin,
dry toasted
2 teaspoons salt
freshly ground pepper to taste

Pulse the cannelloni beans in a food processor for a few seconds or just until half the beans are mashed. Add the tomatoes, parsley, garlic, olive oil, lemon juice, cumin, salt and pepper. Pulse until well combined, adding water if needed for the desired consistency.

Taste and adjust the lemon juice, salt and pepper. Spoon into a serving bowl and serve with Garlic Pita Chips or fresh vegetables.

You may substitute fresh cannelloni beans for the canned beans.

Serves 10

Herbed Cheese

THANKS TO ECKERT'S COUNTRY STORE

1 small garlic clove
1 green onion, chopped
1/4 cup fresh basil leaves
1/4 cup fresh parsley leaves
1 tablespoon fresh oregano, or
1/2 teaspoon dried oregano
8 ounces cream cheese,
softened
1 tablespoon milk

Combine the garlic, green onion, basil, parsley and oregano in a blender or food processor and process until finely chopped. Add the cream cheese and milk and process until smooth. Spoon into a small dish and chill, covered, for 24 hours or longer to blend the flavors. Serve with crackers.

Serves 6 to 8

Guacamole

THANKS TO THE KELLY TWINS

1   jalapeño chile, minced
1/4 cup minced red onion
1   garlic clove, minced
3/4 teaspoon cumin seeds, toasted
     and ground
3/4 teaspoon salt, or to taste
2   tablespoons extra-virgin
     olive oil, or to taste
juice of 1 lime, or to taste
2   avocados
hot sauce to taste (optional)

Combine the jalapeño chile, onion and garlic in a large bowl. Add the cumin, salt, olive oil and half the lime juice and mix well. Cut the avocados into halves and discard the seeds. Cube the avocado in the peels and scoop it out of the peels with a spoon, taking care not to mash it any more than necessary. Mix gently and adjust the lime juice and salt to taste. Add the hot sauce.

Serves 4

Hautly Hummus

THANKS TO HAUTLY CHEESE

1   (15-ounce) can chick-peas,
     drained and rinsed
1   garlic clove
1/4 cup lemon juice
1   teaspoon sea salt
2   tablespoons pine nuts
2   tablespoons chopped parsley
1/2 cup (2 ounces) grated Hautly
     Parmesan cheese
olive oil

Combine the chick-peas and garlic in a food processor and process until smooth. Add the lemon juice and sea salt and pulse until mixed. Add the pine nuts, parsley, Parmesan cheese and just enough olive oil to make the desired consistency, mixing well. Serve with vegetables, olives and flatbread.

Hummus is high in protein. Use it as a dip, add it to a baked potato with broccoli or spread it in a tortilla shell with roasted vegetables for a quick meal.

Serves 4

Dining In

Appetizers

Warm Herbed
Goat Cheese Dip

THANKS TO WHOLE FOODS MARKET

2 garlic cloves, finely minced
4 ounces plain mild fresh
   goat cheese
1 fresh rosemary sprig
1/4 cup extra-virgin olive oil

Sprinkle the garlic in a 5×9-inch gratin dish, ramekin or small baking dish that is at least 1 1/2 inches deep. Crumble the goat cheese into the dish and place the rosemary sprig between the cheese and the side of the dish. Press the cheese down with the back to spoon to even the top. Add the olive oil to within 1/8-inch of the top of the dish. Bake at 350 degrees for 10 minutes or until bubbly.

Makes about 1 cup

Layered Lobster Dip

THANKS TO FELIX'S RESTAURANT

4 ounces herbed cream
   cheese, softened
1 tablespoon Thousand Island
   salad dressing
3 ounces lobster claw knuckle
   meat, shrimp or crab meat
2 tablespoons chopped onion
6 tablespoons chopped tomato
2 tablespoons chopped
   green onions
1 hard-cooked egg, chopped
salt and pepper to taste
tortilla chips
chopped fresh parsley or parsley
   flakes for garnish

Spread the cream cheese in a circle in the center of a serving plate. Spread the salad dressing lightly over the cream cheese and top with the lobster meat. Layer the onion, tomato and green onions over the top and sprinkle the eggs around the edge. Season with salt and pepper. Arrange the chips around the outer edge and garnish the edge of the plate with parsley flakes.

Serves 4

Baked Spinach and Artichoke Yogurt Dip

THANKS TO THE ST. LOUIS DAIRY COUNCIL

1 (14-ounce) can artichoke hearts
1 (10-ounce) package frozen chopped spinach, thawed and squeezed dry
1 cup plain low-fat yogurt
1 cup (4 ounces) shredded low-moisture part-skim mozzarella cheese
1/4 cup chopped green onions
1 garlic clove, chopped
2 tablespoons chopped red bell pepper

Drain and chop the artichoke hearts. Combine with the spinach, yogurt, mozzarella cheese, green onions and garlic in a bowl and mix well. Spoon into a 1-quart baking dish or 9-inch pie plate. Bake at 350 degrees for 20 to 25 minutes or until heated through. Sprinkle with the bell pepper and serve.

Serves 8

Veggie Dip

THANKS TO THE MISSOURI EGG COUNCIL

1 cup low-fat sour cream or plain yogurt
1 tablespoon chopped green onions
1 1/2 teaspoons chopped fresh cilantro
1 1/2 teaspoons Worcestershire sauce
1/4 teaspoon hot pepper sauce
1/4 teaspoon garlic powder
1/4 teaspoon salt
3 hard-cooked eggs
fresh cilantro for garnish

Combine the sour cream, green onions, 1 1/2 teaspoons cilantro, the Worcestershire sauce, hot pepper sauce, garlic powder and salt in a bowl and beat until smooth. Slice two center slices from one egg and reserve for the top; chop the remaining eggs. Stir the chopped eggs into the sour cream mixture.

Chill, covered, to blend the flavors. Spoon into a serving dish and top with the reserved egg slices. Garnish with additional cilantro and serve with vegetables for dipping.

Serves 6

Soups & Salads

St. Louis Zoo

When I think of family, I think of love. I want a family who is always there for me. I feel sad when I think of adoption because there are a lot of kids out here looking for a family. To me being adopted means having a family that is willing to love a child in need.

Jessie, age 12, in foster care

Children enter foster care through no fault of their own, but many foster children blame themselves. This often results in low self-esteem. Jessie's Little Wish was to attend dance camp. Shy at first, Jessie carefully watched the dance pros, studying every step. Now she's center stage, dazzling the audience with her confidence and talent.

Chilled Strawberry Soup

2 cups sliced fresh strawberries
1 cup orange juice
1 cup plain yogurt
1 tablespoon sugar
1/2 teaspoon vanilla extract
3/4 cup Champagne or sparkling
white grape juice
strawberries for garnish

Combine the strawberries, orange juice, yogurt, sugar and vanilla in a blender and process until smooth. Spoon into a bowl and chill in the refrigerator. Stir in the Champagne at serving time and ladle into soup bowls. Garnish with additional strawberries.

Serves 4

Beer Cheese Soup

4 ribs celery, chopped
1 yellow onion, chopped
3 carrots, chopped
1 green bell pepper, chopped
1/2 cup (1 stick) butter
1 1/2 quarts beer
4 quarts heavy cream or
half-and-half
3 1/2 pounds shredded mixture of
Cheddar cheese and Monterey
Jack cheese

Sauté the celery, onion, carrots and bell pepper in the butter in a large saucepan until tender. Add the beer and bring the mixture to a boil. Stir in the cream and cheese. Reduce the heat and simmer for 30 minutes, stirring occasionally. Ladle into soup bowls.

Makes 1 1/2 gallons

"4th and Goal"
Hot Brat Soup

THANKS TO THE CLEVER CLEAVER BROTHERS

1   (5-count) package bratwurst
2   tablespoons olive oil
6   garlic cloves, thinly sliced
1   cup thinly sliced sweet onion
1   cup sliced mushrooms
1   cup sliced carrots
1   tablespoon chili powder
1/4 cup hot sauce
1/4 cup madeira
1   (15-ounce) can white
    beans, drained
1   (15-ounce) can red kidney
    beans, drained
1   cup sliced green onions
1   (15-ounce) can Mexican-style
    stewed tomatoes, sliced
1   quart chicken stock
salt and pepper to taste
juice of 1 lemon
16 slices French bread
olive oil
1   cup (4 ounces) shredded
    Parmesan cheese

Place the bratwurst on a grill heated to medium-low. Grill for 25 to 30 minutes or until cooked through and golden brown. Remove from the grill and slice into bite-size pieces.

Heat 2 tablespoons olive oil in a 3-quart stockpot. Add the garlic and sauté for 30 seconds. Add the onion, mushrooms, carrots and chili powder. Sauté for 2 minutes and stir in the hot sauce, wine, white beans, kidney beans, green onions, tomatoes, bratwurst, chicken stock, salt and pepper. Bring to a boil and reduce the heat to a simmer. Cook for 10 minutes. Stir in the lemon juice.

Brush both sides of the French bread with additional olive oil and grill until toasted. Ladle the soup into bowls and top with the Parmesan cheese. Serve with the toasted bread.

This recipe was tested with Johnsonville Brats Original Bratwurst and Cholula Hot Sauce.

Serves 6 to 8

Dining In

Dining In

Chicken Tortilla Soup

THANKS TO BAHAMA BREEZE

1   tablespoon olive oil
1   cup (1/2-inch pieces) chopped
     calabasa or pumpkin
1/2 cup (1/2-inch pieces) chopped
     red onion
2   teaspoons sliced seeded
     jalapeño chile
1   teaspoon chopped garlic
8   cups canned chicken broth
1 1/2 cups drained canned corn
1   cup (1/2-inch pieces) jicama
1   cup (1/2-inch pieces) chopped
     tomato
salt to taste
1/4 cup fresh lime juice
1   teaspoon chopped oregano
1   pound chicken breast, cooked
     and sliced
Tortilla Soup Toppings (below)

Heat the olive oil in a large saucepan and add the calabasa, onion, jalapeño chile and garlic. Sauté until tender-crisp. Add the chicken broth, corn, jicama and tomato. Bring to a boil and reduce the heat. Simmer until the calabasa is tender. Season with salt and stir in the lime juice, oregano and chicken. Simmer for 5 minutes. Ladle into soup bowls. Serve with Tortilla Soup Toppings.

Serves 6 to 8

Tortilla Soup Toppings

4   (6-inch) blue corn tortillas
4   (6-inch) white corn tortillas
1   cup canola oil or peanut oil
salt to taste
1/2 cup (1/2-inch pieces)
     chopped avocado
8   teaspoons chopped
     fresh cilantro
1/2 cup (1/2-inch pieces)
     chopped avocado

Cut the tortillas into halves in a cutting board and then into strips 1/8 inch wide. Heat the canola oil in a small saucepan and add the strips in batches, frying until crisp. Drain on paper towels.

Serves 6 to 8

Santa Fe Chicken Soup

2 tablespoons butter
1 onion, chopped
6 ribs celery, chopped
2 large carrots, chopped
1 Anaheim chile, chopped
1 small red or green bell
  pepper, chopped
1 1/2 teaspoons crushed toasted
  cumin seeds
1/2 teaspoon dried thyme leaves
1 teaspoon chile powder
1 (49-ounce) can chicken broth
1 (14-ounce) can diced
  tomatoes, drained
2 tablespoons tomato paste
1 cup frozen corn
1 pound chicken breasts, cooked
  and chopped
1 (15-ounce) can black beans,
  drained and rinsed
2 tablespoons chopped
  fresh cilantro
4 ounces uncooked fideos
dash of Tabasco sauce
salt, cayenne pepper and black
  pepper to taste
1 large avocado, chopped
2 tablespoons chopped
  fresh cilantro

Melt the butter in a Dutch oven or large stockpot over medium heat. Add the onion, celery, carrots, Anaheim chile and bell pepper and sauté for 5 minutes, stirring occasionally. Stir in the cumin, thyme and chile powder and sauté for 1 minute. Add the chicken broth, tomatoes, tomato paste and corn. Bring to a boil and reduce the heat. Simmer for 20 minutes.

Stir in the chicken, black beans, 2 tablespoons cilantro and the pasta. Cook just until the noodles are tender. Season with Tabasco sauce, salt, cayenne pepper and black pepper. Ladle into soup bowls and top evenly with the avocado and 2 tablespoons cilantro. Serve with tortilla chips and salsa or corn bread.

You can cool the soup completely, spoon into freezer containers, and freeze for up to 4 months.

Serves 8

Chunky Vegetable Soup

THANKS TO HAUTLY CHEESE

2 teaspoons olive oil
1 cup chopped onion
1 cup sliced mushrooms
1 cup chopped carrots
1 cup chopped green bell pepper
1 teaspoon each thyme,
   rosemary, basil and sage
1/4 teaspoon pepper
1 (14-ounce) can vegetable broth
1 (15-ounce) can no-salt-added
   diced tomatoes
1 (15-ounce) can navy beans,
   drained and rinsed
Crispy Cheese Crackers (below)

Heat the olive oil in a Dutch oven over medium-high heat. Add the onion, mushrooms, carrots and bell pepper. Cover and cook for 3 minutes. Stir in the thyme, rosemary, basil, sage, pepper, vegetable broth and undrained tomatoes. Bring to a boil and reduce the heat. Simmer, covered, for 5 minutes. Stir in the navy beans and simmer, covered, for 5 minutes longer.

Ladle the soup into soup bowls and top with Crispy Cheese Crackers.

You can use an immersion blender to purée a portion of the vegetables before adding the navy beans for a thicker soup.

Serves 6

Crispy Cheese Crackers

THANKS TO HAUTLY CHEESE

1 Hautly Asiago Cheese Wedge

Shred the cheese with a medium shredder. Sprinkle 1/2 cup of the cheese in a thin even layer on a baking parchment-lined baking sheet. Bake at 350 degrees for 5 to 7 minutes or until golden brown. Cool for 4 to 5 minutes and break into bite-size pieces.

Serves 6

Black Bean Chili

1 pound ground bison or lean ground beef
1 pound Italian sausage, casings removed
1 yellow onion, chopped
1 green bell pepper, chopped
1 garlic clove, chopped
2 (14-ounce) cans diced tomatoes
1 (14-ounce) can black beans, drained and rinsed
2 cubes beef bouillon, or 2 ounces beef base
1 tablespoon cider vinegar
2 teaspoons prepared mustard
2 to 3 tablespoons chili powder
1 teaspoon dried oregano leaves
2 teaspoons ground cumin
1/2 teaspoon crushed red pepper flakes (optional)
1/4 to 1/2 teaspoon black pepper

Sauté the bison and sausage in a medium saucepan until brown and crumbly. Drain in a strainer. Return to the saucepan and add the onion, bell pepper and garlic. Sauté until the onion is tender.

Stir in the undrained tomatoes, black beans, beef bouillon cubes, vinegar, mustard, chili powder, oregano, cumin, red pepper flakes and black pepper. Bring to a simmer and simmer for 30 to 45 minutes or until the desired consistency. Ladle into serving bowls.

Serves 4 to 6

Dining In

To date, there have been six hosts of the show; they are John Pertzborn, Debbye Turner, Dan Buck, Kelly Jackson, Chris Balish, and Heidi Glaus.

Dining In

Championship Chili

1   tablespoon olive oil
1 1/2 pounds ground turkey
8   ounces bulk Italian sausage
1   envelope chili seasoning
1   cup chopped red onion
1/2 cup chopped red bell pepper
1   (14-ounce) can beef broth
1   (4-ounce) can chopped
    green chiles, drained
2   tablespoons lime juice
1   cup medium-hot picante sauce
1   (15-ounce) can cannelloni
    beans or navy beans,
    drained and rinsed
1   (15-ounce) can black beans,
    drained and rinsed

Heat the olive oil in a 4-quart saucepan over medium heat. Add the turkey and sausage. Cook until brown, stirring until crumbly; drain. Add the chili seasoning, onion and bell pepper and cook for 3 to 4 minutes or until the vegetable are tender-crisp, stirring frequently. Add the broth, green chiles, lime juice and picante sauce. Bring to a boil and reduce the heat. Simmer for 15 minutes. Stir in the cannelloni beans and black beans. Simmer for 5 to 10 minutes or until heated through. Ladle into soup bowls.

Serves 6 to 8

The *Show Me St. Louis* staff has collectively
won more than fifteen Emmy Awards™ over the
past eleven years.

Famous White Chili

1   tablespoon olive oil
2   onions, chopped
4   garlic cloves, minced
2   (4-ounce) cans chopped mild
    green chiles
2   teaspoons ground cumin
1 1/2 teaspoons crumbled dried
    oregano leaves
1/4 teaspoon cayenne pepper
    (optional)
3   (16-ounce) cans
    Great Northern white beans
6   cups chicken stock or canned
    chicken broth
4   cups chopped cooked
    chicken breast
3   cups (12 ounces) shredded
    Monterey Jack cheese
salt and pepper to taste
sour cream for garnish

Heat the olive oil in a large heavy saucepan over medium-high heat. Add the onions and sauté for 10 minutes or until the onions are translucent. Stir in the garlic, green chiles, cumin, oregano and cayenne pepper. Sauté for 2 minutes.

Add the undrained beans and chicken stock and bring to a boil. Add the chicken and cheese and cook until the cheese melts, stirring constantly. Season with salt and pepper and ladle into serving bowls. Garnish with sour cream.

Serves 6

Holiday Meatball Soup

THANKS TO DOMINIC'S

1 small onion, chopped
3 tablespoons olive oil
1 small carrot, chopped
1 tomato, peeled and chopped
2 garlic cloves, finely chopped
2 ounces fresh spinach, chopped
7 cups beef broth or chicken
broth, heated
salt and pepper to taste
Italian Meatballs (below)
1/4 cup white wine
2 cups cooked rice
3 tablespoons chopped
fresh parsley
1/4 cup (1 ounce) grated
Parmesan cheese

Sauté the onion in the heated olive oil in a medium saucepan for 10 minutes. Add the carrot, tomato, garlic and spinach. Cook over medium heat for 5 minutes, stirring frequently.

Add the hot beef broth and mix well. Season with salt and pepper. Bring to a boil and add the Italian Meatballs and wine; reduce the heat and simmer for 2 minutes. Stir in the rice and sprinkle with the parsley. Let stand for several minutes and ladle into soup bowls. Serve with the Parmesan cheese.

Serves 6

Italian Meatballs

7 ounces lean ground beef
1 egg
1/4 cup bread crumbs
1/4 cup (1 ounce) grated
Parmesan cheese
salt and pepper to taste

Combine the ground beef, egg, bread crumbs, Parmesan cheese, salt and pepper in a bowl and mix well. Shape into very small meatballs and arrange in a baking pan. Bake at 400 degrees for 5 minutes.

Serves 6

Black Bean Salad

1 (30-ounce) can black
  beans, drained and rinsed
1/2 red onion, finely chopped
1 cup chopped Roma tomatoes
2 garlic cloves, finely minced
1 small jalapeño chile, minced
1/4 cup extra-virgin olive oil
1 tablespoon lime juice
salt and freshly ground pepper
  to taste
1/2 cup chopped fresh cilantro

Combine the beans with the onion, tomatoes, garlic and jalapeño chile in a large bowl and mix well. Whisk the olive oil and lime juice together in a small bowl. Add to the bean mixture and mix gently. Season to taste with salt and pepper. Chill, covered, for 4 hours or longer. Stir in the cilantro just before serving.

Serves 6

Dining In

To date, there have been five reporters on the show; they are Wendy Bell, Dan Buck, Wendy Erickson, Heidi Glaus, and Jim Schugel.

Roasted Pear Salad

THANKS TO THE KELLY TWINS

3   Bosc pears or other firm pears
2   tablespoons olive oil
2   tablespoons honey
1   teaspoon chopped fresh thyme
salt and freshly ground pepper
      to taste
6   ounces baby lettuce
1   fennel bulb, thinly sliced
      crosswise
1   (4-ounce) piece of Parmigiano-
      Reggiano cheese, asiago cheese
      or blue cheese
3/4 cup walnuts, lightly toasted and
      skins removed
3/4 cup extra-virgin olive oil
6   tablespoons balsamic vinegar

Peel the pears and cut into halves, discarding the cores. Toss gently with 2 tablespoons olive oil, the honey, thyme, salt and pepper in a bowl. Taste and adjust the seasonings. Place cut side down on a baking sheet lined with foil or baking parchment. Roast at 400 degrees for 15 minutes or until dark golden brown with some spots of deep brown, but still firm; check for doneness with a skewer.

Cut each pear half into long strips 1/4 inch wide and assemble one pear half on each serving plate. Place a handful of baby lettuce and several fennel slices over each pear half, taking care not to cover the pear completely. Shred the cheese over the salads with a vegetable peeler and sprinkle the walnuts on the plates.

Drizzle 2 tablespoons extra-virgin olive oil and 1 tablespoon balsamic vinegar over each salad. Sprinkle with pepper and serve immediately with warm crusty bread.

Serves 6

Strawberry Romaine Salad

THANKS TO ECKERT'S COUNTRY STORE

1 large head romaine
1 pint strawberries, sliced
1 cup (4 ounces) shredded
  Monterey Jack cheese
1/2 cup chopped walnuts, toasted
Red Wine Vinaigrette (below)

Combine the lettuce, strawberries, Monterey Jack cheese and walnuts in a large salad bowl. Shake the Red Wine Vinaigrette well and drizzle over the salad. Toss the salad gently to coat and serve immediately.

Serves 12

Red Wine Vinaigrette

THANKS TO ECKERT'S COUNTRY STORE

1 cup vegetable oil
1/2 cup red wine vinegar
3/4 cup sugar
2 garlic cloves, minced
1/2 teaspoon paprika
1/2 teaspoon salt
1/4 teaspoon white pepper

Combine the oil, vinegar, sugar, garlic, paprika, salt and white pepper in a large jar and shake to mix well. Store in the refrigerator for up to one week.

Makes about 2 cups

Soups & Salads

Mustard-Crusted Steak Salad with Blue Cheese

THANKS TO THE ST. LOUIS DAIRY COUNCIL

3   ounces beef tenderloin, thinly sliced
1   tablespoon Dijon mustard
3   cups baby spinach
1/4 cup (1 ounce) crumbled blue cheese
1   slice red onion, separated into rings
3   cherry tomatoes
2   mushrooms, sliced
1   tablespoon balsamic vinegar
1   teaspoon olive oil
1   tablespoon toasted pine nuts (optional)

Spread both sides of the tenderloin slices with a thin layer of the Dijon mustard. Heat a small nonstick skillet over medium-high heat and spray with nonstick cooking spray. Cook the beef for 1 minute on each side or until brown.

Place the spinach on a serving plate and sprinkle with the blue cheese. Arrange the beef slices over the center of the spinach. Arrange the onion rings, tomatoes and mushrooms around the spinach.

Blend the balsamic vinegar and olive oil in a small cup and drizzle over the salad. Top with the pine nuts.

Serves 1

Show Me St. Louis has done more than fifty stories on the St. Louis Zoo.

Tenderloin Salad with Cranberries and Pears

THANKS TO THE MISSOURI BEEF COUNCIL

4 (4-ounce) beef tenderloin
   steaks, cut 3/4 inch thick
1/2 teaspoon coarsely
   ground pepper
1/4 cup coarsely chopped pecans
1 (5-ounce) package mixed baby
   salad greens
1 red or green pear, cored and
   cut into 16 wedges
1/4 cup dried cranberries
salt to taste
Honey Mustard Dressing (below)
1/4 cup (1 ounce) crumbled goat
   cheese (optional)

Season the steaks with the pepper. Heat a large nonstick skillet over medium heat. Add the steaks and cook for 7 to 9 minutes for medium-rare to medium, turning occasionally.

Sprinkle the pecans in a single layer on a baking sheet. Bake at 350 degrees for 3 to 5 minutes or until light brown, stirring occasionally. Cool to room temperature.

Divide the salad greens evenly among four serving plates. Top with the pear wedges and cranberries. Cut the steaks into thin slices and season with salt. Arrange the slices over the salad greens. Drizzle with the Honey Mustard Dressing and sprinkle with the pecans and goat cheese.

Serves 4

Honey Mustard Dressing

THANKS TO THE MISSOURI BEEF COUNCIL

1/2 cup prepared honey mustard
2 to 3 tablespoons water
1 1/2 teaspoons olive oil
1 teaspoon white wine vinegar
1/8 teaspoon salt
1/4 teaspoon coarsely
   ground pepper

Combine the honey mustard, water, olive oil, vinegar, salt and pepper in a small bowl and whisk until smooth. Store in the refrigerator until needed.

Makes 3/4 cup

Dining In

Chicken and Spinach Salad

6 ounces fresh spinach
2 ounces golden raisins
1/2 cup broken walnuts
Balsamic Mustard Dressing (below)
4 ounces grilled chicken breast
3 ounces creamy Brie
   cheese, chopped
strawberries or other fresh fruit
   for garnish

Combine the spinach, raisins and walnuts with the desired amount of Balsamic Mustard Dressing in a bowl and toss to coat evenly. Spoon onto salad plates. Cut the chicken into strips and arrange over the salads. Sprinkle with the Brie cheese and garnish with strawberries.

Serves 4

Balsamic Mustard Dressing

2 cups Italian dressing
1/2 cup balsamic vinegar
3 tablespoons (about)
   Dijon mustard
1/3 cup cabernet sauvignon

Combine the Italian dressing, vinegar, Dijon mustard and wine in a bowl and whisk until smooth. Store in a covered container in the refrigerator until needed.

This recipe was tested with Good Seasons Italian dressing. Do not use creamy Italian dressing.

Makes about 3 cups

Pan–Seared Scallops over Mixed Greens

THANKS TO WHOLE FOODS MARKET

2 tablespoons olive oil
10 sea scallops
salt and pepper to taste
2 tablespoons Whole Foods
    Market Flavored butter
2 tablespoons white wine
2 cups mixed salad greens
1/4 cup lemon tahini dressing

Heat the olive oil in a shallow pan over medium-low to medium heat. Season the scallops with salt and pepper. Sear in the heated pan for 1 to 3 minutes on each side or until brown. Add the butter and wine and cook for 2 minutes to reduce the liquid.

Mix the salad greens and the salad dressing in a bowl and spoon into serving bowls. Place the scallops over the salads.

This recipe was tested using 365 Everyday Value Olive Oil and 365 Organic Everyday Value Lemon Tahini Dressing.

Serves 2

Actress Valerie Harper appeared on
the program in 2002.

Savory Asian Noodle and Walnut Salad

6 cups water
6 ounces vermicelli rice noodles
1/2 cup fat-free Asian-style
 salad dressing
1/2 cup chopped walnuts
1 pound medium shrimp, peeled
 and deveined, about 16 shrimp
salt and pepper to taste
2 tablespoons fat-free Asian-style
 salad dressing
1 red bell pepper, julienned
3/4 cup thinly sliced green onions,
 about 8 to 10 green onions
1 large English cucumber, peeled,
 seeded and thinly sliced
3/4 cup bean sprouts
1 carrot, peeled and julienned
 or grated
1/3 cup chopped fresh cilantro
2 teaspoons grated fresh ginger
4 cups mixed Asian greens, such
 as mizuna, tat soi, red mustard
 and Napa cabbage
1 tablespoon fat-free Asian-style
 salad dressing
1 head butter lettuce
cilantro leaves for garnish

Bring the water to a boil in a saucepan. Add the rice noodles and cook for 3 to 4 minutes or until tender. Drain, cool slightly and toss with 1/2 cup salad dressing in a bowl. Chill in the refrigerator.

Sprinkle the walnuts in a single layer on a baking sheet. Toast at 350 degrees for 5 to 7 minutes or just until light brown. Cool to room temperature.

Season the shrimp lightly with salt and pepper. Thread two shrimp onto each of eight bamboo skewers. Coat a large nonstick skillet with canola nonstick cooking spray and place over medium-high heat. Add the shrimp and sear for 3 minutes on each side. Brush with 2 tablespoons salad dressing. Cool to room temperature.

Toss the chilled rice noodles with half the walnuts, the bell pepper, green onions, cucumber, bean sprouts, carrot, cilantro and ginger in a bowl. Toss the Asian greens with 1 tablespoon salad dressing in a bowl.

Arrange butter lettuce cups on four salad plates. Spoon the Asian greens into the lettuce cups and spoon the rice noodle mixture next to the greens. Top each salad with two shrimp skewers and sprinkle with the remaining walnuts. Garnish with cilantro leaves.

Serves 4

Creamy Egg Salad

THANKS TO THE MISSOURI EGG COUNCIL

1	tablespoon finely chopped onion
1/2	cup mayonnaise
1 1/2	tablespoons lemon juice
2	teaspoons Dijon mustard
1/4	teaspoon hot pepper sauce
1/4	teaspoon seasoned salt
1/8	teaspoon white pepper
3	ounces cream cheese, cubed and softened
6	hard-cooked eggs, chopped

chopped green onion for garnish

Combine the onion, mayonnaise, lemon juice, Dijon mustard, hot pepper sauce, seasoned salt and white pepper in a blender or food processor. Process to mix well. Add the cream cheese and process until smooth. Remove to a medium bowl and fold in the eggs. Garnish with green onion.

Serves 4

Heidi Glaus interviewed Country Music Sensation Gretchen Wilson in 2004.

Dining In

Main Dishes

St. Louis Science Center

I hope for a family everyday. I'd like a family that would sit down and talk with me. I think it is important for everyone to have a family that is there for them. All kids need to belong.

Kameron, age 11, in foster care

Children in foster care are often separated from their brothers and sisters. Kameron's Little Wish
was to go to Six Flags with brothers that he had not seen for many months. They had a wonderful reunion,
experiencing the thrill of the rides and the delight of precious time spent together.

Espresso-Crusted Beef Roast

THANKS TO THE MISSOURI BEEF COUNCIL

1   tablespoon ground
    espresso beans
1   tablespoon brown sugar
1   teaspoon salt
1   teaspoon coarsely
    ground pepper
1   (4- to 6-pound) small-end
    beef rib-eye roast
Balsamic Sauce (below)

Combine the ground espresso, brown sugar, salt and pepper in a small bowl; mix well. Press the mixture evenly over the roast. Place the roast fat side up on a rack in a shallow roasting pan and insert a meat thermometer into the thickest portion, not resting on fat. Roast, uncovered, at 350 degrees for $1^3/4$ to 2 hours for medium-rare, 135 degrees on the meat thermometer, or for 2 to $2^1/2$ hours for medium, 150 degrees on the meat thermometer.

Remove to a cutting board and tent loosely with foil, leaving the meat thermometer inserted. Let stand for 15 minutes; the temperature will continue to rise about 10 degrees. Skim the fat from the drippings and reserve the drippings for the sauce. Carve the roast into thin slices. Serve with Balsamic Sauce.

Serves 6 to 8

Balsamic Sauce

THANKS TO THE MISSOURI BEEF COUNCIL

1   cup balsamic vinegar
$1/4$ cup cider vinegar
1   cup beef broth
reserved roast drippings
$1/4$ teaspoon coarsely
    ground pepper
$1/4$ cup ($1/2$ stick) butter, softened
4   teaspoons all-purpose flour

Bring the balsamic vinegar and cider vinegar to a boil in a small nonreactive saucepan over medium heat. Cook for 20 minutes or until reduced to $1/4$ cup. Add the beef broth, reserved roast drippings and pepper. Blend the butter and flour in a small bowl. Whisk gradually into the sauce. Bring the sauce to a boil, whisking constantly. Reduce the heat and simmer for 1 minute, stirring constantly.

Serves 6 to 8

Peppered Fillet with
Cognac Sauce

THANKS TO SOULARD'S RESTAURANT

1/4 cup chopped onion
2   tablespoons minced garlic
1/2 cup (1 stick) butter, melted
1   small carrot, thinly julienned
1 1/2 cups sliced mushrooms
2   teaspoons Worcestershire sauce
2   teaspoons salt
2   teaspoons pepper
1 1/2 cups cup beef broth
1/4 cup Cognac
2   tablespoons all-purpose flour
1/4 cup heavy cream
4   (8-ounce) beef tenderloin steaks
2   tablespoons seasoned salt
1/4 cup partially cracked pepper

Sauté the onion and garlic in the butter in a heavy saucepan just until tender. Add the carrot, mushrooms, Worcestershire sauce, salt and pepper. Sauté until the mushrooms are tender.

Add the beef broth and Cognac. Stir in the flour and bring to a boil, stirring constantly. Reduce the heat and add the cream. Simmer until reduced to the desired consistency. Keep warm.

Season the steaks on both sides with the seasoned salt and cracked pepper. Grill until done to taste. Serve with the sauce.

This recipe was tested with Lawry's seasoned salt.

Serves 4

Dining In

Only 10 percent of the video we shoot actually makes air.

Filet Mignon with Pinot Noir Sauce

1 teaspoon vegetable oil
2 tablespoons finely
  chopped shallots
1/4 cup sun-dried cherries
1 cup pinot noir
1 cup veal or beef demi-glace
2 tablespoons butter
salt and ground pepper to taste
1 filet mignon
cracked pepper to taste
deep-fried carrots strips and/or thinly
  sliced baked potato for garnish

Heat the vegetable oil in a sauté pan over medium heat. Add the shallots and sauté for 5 minutes or until tender. Add the cherries and sauté for 2 minutes. Add the wine and bring to a boil. Cook until reduced by two-thirds. Stir in the demi-glace and cook until reduced by one-half or until the consistency of a thin syrup. Remove from the heat and whisk in the butter. Season with salt and ground pepper.

Roll the steak in cracked pepper. Grill or boil for 8 to 12 minutes on each side or until done to taste. Serve with the wine sauce. Garnish with the carrot strips and/or potato slices.

Serves 1

Beef Tenderloin Penne

THANKS TO THE CRAZY FISH FRESH GRILL

5 ounces beef tenderloin, sliced
2 tablespoons red wine
6 tablespoons beef stock
6 ounces penne, cooked
2 portobello mushrooms, roasted
  and sliced
1 red bell pepper, roasted
  and sliced
1/4 cup chopped tomato
2 tablespoons chopped scallions
1 teaspoon chopped fresh thyme
kosher salt and pepper to taste
2 ounces blue cheese, crumbled
1/4 cup (1 ounce) grated
  Parmesan cheese

Pan-roast the beef tenderloin in a large skillet just until cooked through. Add the wine and beef stock, stirring to deglaze the skillet. Add the pasta, mushrooms, bell pepper, tomato, scallions and thyme. Cook for 2 minutes. Season with kosher salt and pepper. Top with the blue cheese and Parmesan cheese and serve immediately.

Serves 2

Tenderloin Brochette
with Wild Rice

THANKS TO DOMINIC'S

3	garlic cloves
32	ounces beef tenderloin, cut into large chunks
1/2	cup (about) Italian bread crumbs
1/4	cup (1 ounce) grated Romano cheese
1/2	teaspoon chopped parsley
1/4	cup extra-virgin olive oil
2	tablespoons red wine
2	tablespoons Worcestershire sauce

salt and pepper to taste
Wild Rice (below)
chopped parsley for garnish

Crush the garlic in a large bowl. Add the beef, bread crumbs, Romano cheese and 1 teaspoon parsley. Stir in the olive oil, wine, Worcestershire sauce, salt and pepper; toss to coat evenly. Marinate in the refrigerator for several hours.

Thread the beef onto skewers and grill until done to taste. Spoon Wild Rice onto a serving platter and top with the beef. Garnish with parsley.

This recipe was tested with Lea & Perrins Worcestershire sauce.

Serves 4

Wild Rice

THANKS TO DOMINIC'S

12	ounces uncooked wild rice
1/4	cup olive oil
1/4	onion, chopped
8	ounces chopped fresh vegetables, such as zucchini, carrots, broccoli, peas and/or mushrooms
1/4	cup (1/2 stick) butter
2	cups beef broth

salt and pepper to taste

Cook the rice using the package directions. Rinse in cold water and drain. Heat the olive oil in a large skillet and add the onion. Sauté for 5 minutes or until translucent. Add the chopped vegetables, butter and beef broth and cook for 10 minutes. Add the rice and mix gently; cook just until heated through. Season with salt and pepper.

Serves 4

Main Dishes

Chilled Blackened Tenderloin with Hearts of Palm

THANKS TO MIKE SHANNON'S RESTAURANT

1   (8-ounce) beef tenderloin
1   tablespoon Cajun seasoning
4   slices hearts of palm
2   midget sweet pickles
2   pepperoncini
2   strips roasted red pepper

Season the beef well with the Cajun seasoning. Insert a meat thermometer into the thickest portion. Grill or roast the beef to 130 degrees on the meat thermometer. Chill the beef for 8 to 24 hours. Chill the hearts of palm, pickles, pepperoncini and roasted red peppers for 4 hours or longer. Place the tenderloin on a plate and arrange the chilled vegetables around the beef.

You may cut the tenderloin in half and share the other ingredients between two persons for appetizer servings.

Serves 1 as a main dish or 2 as an appetizer

Beef Tenderloin Flatbread

THANKS TO CRAZY FISH FRESH GRILL

olive oil
4   ounces sliced grilled
    beef tenderloin
2   ounces roasted herbed
    potatoes
2   ounces caramelized onion
1   (6-inch) pita flatbread
1   ounce creamed horseradish
3   slices provolone cheese

Heat a skillet coated with a small amount of olive oil. Sauté the sliced beef briefly in the hot oil. Add the potatoes and onion and sauté until heated through.

Warm the flatbread in an ungreased heated skillet or grill until warm and marked on both sides. Spread with the horseradish and layer with the provolone cheese. Add the beef mixture and cut into quarters to serve.

Serves 1

Sirloin Fajitas

THANKS TO THE MISSOURI BEEF COUNCIL

2 tablespoons fresh lime juice
2 teaspoons canola oil
2 large garlic cloves, minced
1 pound boneless beef top sirloin
  steak or top round steak,
  cut 3/4 inch thick and trimmed
8 (6-inch) fat-free or low-fat
  whole wheat flour tortillas
Tomato Lime Salsa (below)

Mix the lime juice, canola oil and garlic in a plastic bag or glass dish. Add the beef, turning to coat well. Seal the bag or cover the dish and marinate in the refrigerator for 20 to 30 minutes, turning once.

Spray a broiler rack and pan with nonstick cooking spray. Drain the beef, discarding the marinade. Arrange the beef on the rack and place 2 to 3 inches from the heat source in a preheated broiler. Broil for 9 to 12 minutes for a medium-rare top sirloin steak or for 12 to 13 minutes for a medium-rare top round steak, turning occasionally. Cut the steak crosswise into thin slices.

Warm the tortillas using the package directions. Serve the steak in the tortillas and top with Tomato Lime Salsa.

Serves 4

Tomato Lime Salsa

THANKS TO THE MISSOURI BEEF COUNCIL

1 large tomato, seeded, chopped
  and drained, about 1 cup
1/2 cup chopped zucchini
1/4 cup chopped fresh cilantro
1/4 cup prepared salsa
1 tablespoon fresh lime juice

Combine the tomato, zucchini, cilantro, salsa and lime juice in a bowl and mix well. Serve with Sirloin Fajitas.

Serves 4

Main Dishes

Beef Stew

THANKS TO KILKENNY'S PUB

4   pounds beef chuck
salt and pepper to taste
1/4   cup flour
vegetable oil for browning
3   cups chopped onion
2   cups chopped celery
2   cups chopped carrots
2   cups chopped turnips
2   tablespoons tomato paste
1 1/4 cups red wine
1   quart brown veal stock
6   sprigs fresh thyme
4   ounces peas

Season the beef with salt and pepper and coat with the flour. Brown in a small amount of hot oil in a saucepan. Remove the beef with a slotted spoon. Add the onions, celery, carrots and turnips to the drippings in the saucepan and sauté until the onions are brown. Add the tomato paste and cook for 5 minutes, stirring to coat the vegetables well.

Return the beef to the saucepan and add the wine, stirring to deglaze the pan. Cook until the wine has evaporated. Stir in the veal stock, thyme, salt and pepper and bring to a simmer. Simmer until the beef is very tender. Adjust the seasonings to taste and stir in the peas just before serving time.

Serves 8

Pieces of the original *Show Me St. Louis* set were made from the old *Sally Jesse Raphael Show* set.

Herbed Lasagna

1 1/2 pounds lean ground beef
3 tablespoons olive oil
1 1/2 cups finely chopped
   white onions
2 teaspoons chopped garlic
2 cups chopped tomatoes
1 cup tomato sauce
1/2 cup tomato paste
1 tablespoon dried basil
1/2 teaspoon sage
1/4 teaspoon rosemary
1 teaspoon Tabasco sauce
1 teaspoon salt
1/4 teaspoon freshly ground pepper
10 ounces lasagna noodles
4 cups (16 ounces) shredded
   mozzarella cheese
1 cup (4 ounces) grated
   Parmigiano–Reggiano cheese
1 pound fresh spinach leaves,
   finely chopped
12 ounces ricotta cheese

Cook the ground beef in a large skillet over medium-high heat, stirring until brown and crumbly. Remove the beef with a slotted spoon and drain. Add the olive oil and onions to the drippings in the skillet and sauté for 1 minute. Add the garlic and sauté for 2 minutes. Return the ground beef to the skillet and add the tomatoes, tomato sauce, tomato paste, basil, sage, rosemary, Tabasco sauce, salt and pepper. Reduce the heat to low and simmer for 30 minutes or until thickened to the desired consistency.

Cook the lasagna noodles using the package directions. Drain, rinse under cold water and drain again, keeping the noodles separated.

Spread a thin layer of the meat sauce in a buttered 9×13-inch baking pan. Arrange half the lasagna noodles in the pan and top with one-third of the mozzarella cheese and one-third of the Parmigiano-Reggiano cheese.

Mix the spinach with the ricotta cheese in a large bowl. Spread half the mixture over the cheese layer. Layer half the remaining meat sauce, the remaining noodles, half the remaining cheeses and the remaining spinach mixture in the pan. Top with the remaining meat sauce and cheeses.

Bake the lasagna at 375 degrees for 1 hour or until hot and bubbly. Let rest for 15 minutes, and then cut into squares to serve. Serve with additional Parmigiano-Reggiano cheese.

You may wrap the unbaked lasagna in foil, place in a freezer bag, and freeze for later use. Thaw in the refrigerator for 24 hours before baking or bake frozen, covered with the foil for 1 hour and uncovered until bubbly.

Serves 8

Not-Your-Mom's Meat Loaf

5   pounds ground chuck
1   pound yellow onions,
    finely chopped
8   ounces celery, finely chopped
2   tablespoons finely
    chopped garlic
6   eggs
3   cups bread crumbs
Meat Loaf Glaze (below)
2   tablespoons Worcestershire
    sauce
2   tablespoons A-1 steak sauce
3/4 cup ketchup
1/2 tablespoon thyme
1/2 tablespoon marjoram
1/2 tablespoon oregano
2   tablespoons salt

Combine the ground chuck, onions and celery in a large bowl and mix well. Add the garlic, eggs, bread crumbs, 1/4 cup of the Meat Loaf Glaze, the Worcestershire sauce, A-1 sauce, ketchup, thyme, marjoram, oregano and salt and mix just until combined.

Pack the mixture into a large loaf pan and tap on a counter to remove any air bubbles. Spread half the remaining Meat Loaf Glaze over the top and cover with foil. Bake for 13/4 hours. Brush with the remaining glaze and bake for 15 minutes longer. Let stand for 15 minutes before serving.

Serves 12

Meat Loaf Glaze

4   ounces brown sugar
1   cup ketchup
2   tablespoons apple cider vinegar
1/2 tablespoon dry mustard

Combine the brown sugar, ketchup, cider vinegar and dry mustard in a bowl and mix well.

Serves 12

Veal Fontina with Mushrooms

THANKS TO DOMINIC'S

1 pound veal scallops,
1/4 inch thick
1/2 cup all-purpose flour
salt and pepper to taste
butter
1/2 pint mushrooms, sliced
1/2 cup dry white wine
1/2 to 1 cup beef broth
8 ounces fontina cheese,
thinly sliced
2 teaspoons chopped
fresh parsley

Pound the veal thin on a work surface with a meat mallet. Mix the flour with the salt and pepper on a plate. Coat the veal lightly on both sides with the flour mixture, shaking off the excess. Heat butter in a large skillet and add the veal in batches if necessary. Cook until brown on both sides. Remove to a warm ovenproof serving plate.

Add the mushrooms, wine and beef broth to the skillet, stirring to deglaze the bottom. Simmer for 10 minutes. Season with salt and pepper. Spoon the mushroom mixture over the veal and top each serving with a slice of fontina cheese. Broil just until the cheese melts. Sprinkle with the parsley and serve immediately.

Serves 4

Wendy Erikson started out at KSDK as a
news reporter in 1995.

Dining In

Stuffed Veal Breast

THANKS TO DOMINIC'S

8   ounces fresh spinach, trimmed
salt to taste
2   eggs
1   garlic clove, chopped
2   tablespoons pine nuts
1/2   cup (2 ounces) grated
    Parmesan cheese
pepper to taste
1   pound veal breast
2   ounces thinly sliced prosciutto
1/2   cup all-purpose flour
2   tablespoons olive oil
2   tablespoons butter
2   sprigs sage
2   sprigs rosemary
1/2   cup dry white wine
1/2   cup beef stock

Cook the spinach in a small amount of salted water in a saucepan just until tender; drain well and cool. Combine the spinach with the eggs, garlic, pine nuts, Parmesan cheese, salt and pepper in a bowl and mix well.

Pound the veal 1/4 inch thick on a work surface with a meat mallet. Season the veal lightly with salt and spread the spinach mixture over the entire surface of the veal. Top with the prosciutto slices and roll the veal to enclose the filling; secure with kitchen twine. Coat lightly with the flour.

Heat the olive oil and butter in a skillet over medium heat and add the sage and rosemary. Sauté for several minutes. Add the veal and brown on all sides. Add the wine and beef stock and season with salt. Cook for 10 minutes.

Place the veal in a roasting pan and roast, covered, at 350 degrees for 35 minutes, turning every 10 minutes and adding a small amount of additional beef stock if needed to maintain moistness. Increase the oven temperature to 400 degrees and roast, uncovered, for 10 minutes longer. Remove to a serving plate, remove the twine and slice to serve.

Serves 4

Roast Lamb alla Romana

THANKS TO DOMINIC'S

1/2 leg of lamb, about 3 pounds
3 garlic cloves, cut into thin slivers
1 tablespoon olive oil
1 1/2 teaspoons chopped
    fresh rosemary
salt and freshly ground pepper
    to taste
1/2 cup red wine
2 cups vegetable stock
1 small onion, coarsely chopped
1 1/2 pounds potatoes,
    cut into quarters
1 tablespoon olive oil
1 1/2 teaspoons chopped
    fresh rosemary
1 pound baby carrots, cooked

Make deep slits in the lamb with the point of a sharp knife and insert the garlic slivers into the slits. Rub the lamb all over with 1 tablespoon olive oil and place in a roasting pan. Sprinkle with 1 1/2 teaspoons rosemary and season with salt and pepper. Roast at 450 degrees for 30 minutes, turning once.

Reduce the heat to 375 degrees and add the wine, vegetable stock and onion to the roasting pan. Roast for 1 1/4 hours longer or until tender, turning several times and basting after each turn.

Combine the potatoes with 1 tablespoon olive oil and 1 1/2 teaspoons rosemary in a second roasting pan. Season with salt and pepper. Place in the oven 45 minutes before the lamb is done and roast with the lamb until golden brown and tender, turning several times.

Remove the lamb to a cutting board and tent with foil. Let stand in a warm place for 5 minutes. Cut into thin slices and arrange on a large platter. Arrange the potatoes and carrots around the lamb. Strain the cooking juices and spoon over the lamb to serve.

Serves 6

Pork Tenderloin with Raspberry Sauce

4 cups vegetable oil
1/4 cup soy sauce
1 tablespoon onion powder
1/4 cup honey
1 tablespoon garlic powder
4 pork tenderloins, trimmed
seasoned salt and cracked pepper
    to taste
Raspberry Sauce (below)
fresh parsley for garnish

Combine the oil, soy sauce, onion powder, honey and garlic powder in a large sealable plastic bag. Add the pork and marinate in the refrigerator for 8 to 24 hours. Drain, discarding the marinade.

Season the pork with seasoned salt and pepper. Grill for 3 minutes on each side. Remove from the grill and cut into medallions. Grill until done to taste. Serve with Raspberry Sauce. Garnish with fresh parsley.

This recipe was tested with Lawry's seasoned salt.

Serves 16

Raspberry Sauce

1 (16-ounce) jar red
    raspberry preserves
1/4 cup red wine vinegar
1/4 cup ketchup
4 teaspoons soy sauce
2 teaspoons prepared horseradish
1 teaspoon garlic powder

Combine the raspberry preserves, vinegar, ketchup, soy sauce, horseradish and garlic powder in a saucepan. Cook until heated through, stirring to mix well.

Makes 2 1/2 cups

Pan-Seared Pork Mignon

THANKS TO THE ADAM'S MARK HOTEL

4   (6-ounce) center-cut pork
    loin fillets
salt and pepper to taste
1/2   cup all-purpose flour
1/2   cup olive oil
1   cup cremini mushrooms
minced garlic to taste
olive oil for sautéing
1/2   cup demi-glace
1/4   cup port
48   slices rosemary-roasted small
    red potatoes
12   ounces green beans, sautéed
1   cup sautéed sliced
    Bermuda onion
1/4   cup rosemary oil
1   cup crisp tobacco onions
4   sprigs rosemary
4   sprigs thyme

Season the pork with salt and pepper and coat with the flour. Heat 1/2 cup olive oil in a large skillet and add the pork. Cook until brown on both sides. Insert a meat thermometer into the thickest portion of one fillet and place in a roasting pan. Roast at 350 degrees to an internal temperature of 150 degrees.

Sauté the mushrooms with garlic in a small amount of olive oil in a skillet. Add the demi-glace and cook until reduced. Stir in the wine.

Arrange the roasted potatoes in a circle on a serving platter. Spoon the green beans and Bermuda onion into the center of the potatoes and arrange the pork over the top. Spoon the mushroom mixture over the pork and drizzle with the rosemary oil. Top with the tobacco onions, rosemary and thyme.

Serves 4

Dining In

Main Dishes

Barbecued Baby Back Ribs

3   pounds baby back pork ribs
1   tablespoon brown sugar
1   tablespoon paprika
2   teaspoons garlic powder
1 1/2 teaspoons pepper
1/2 cup water
1 1/2 cups barbecue sauce

Cut each rack of ribs into thirds. Arrange half the ribs in a single layer on each of two 18×24-inch sheets of heavy-duty foil. Mix the brown sugar, paprika, garlic powder and pepper in a cup. Sprinkle and rub the mixture over the ribs, turning to coat evenly. Bring opposite sides of the foil to the center and fold the foil to seal the packet, leaving space for the heat to circulate in the packet. Fold in and seal one end of the foil. Pour the water into the packets through the open end and fold to seal that end.

Place on a grill heated to medium and grill, covered, for 45 to 60 minutes. Remove the ribs carefully from the packets and place directly on the grill. Brush generously with the barbecue sauce and grill, uncovered, for 10 to 15 minutes longer or until done to taste, turning every 5 minutes.

You can substitute 3 or 4 ice cubes for the water in the packets if preferred.

Serves 6

The three photojournalists who work on
Show Me St. Louis have fifty years
of experience among them.

Porterhouse Pork Chops

1/2 cup sugar
1/2 cup kosher salt
2 quarts water
3 garlic cloves
1 cinnamon stick
1/4 to 1/2 cup chopped fresh herbs,
    such as basil and thyme
1 teaspoon black peppercorns
4 (16-ounce) Porterhouse-cut
    pork chops
olive oil
Apple Verjus (below)
freshly ground pepper and fresh
    herbs for garnish

Combine the sugar, kosher salt and water in a bowl, stirring to dissolve the sugar and salt. Add the garlic, cinnamon stick, 1/4 cup herbs and the peppercorns. Add the pork chops, coating well. Marinate, covered, in the refrigerator for 4 to 24 hours.

Remove the pork chops from the marinade and brush very lightly with olive oil or spray with nonstick cooking spray; do not use additional salt. Grill over hot coals for 5 minutes on each side. Remove the pork chops to a roasting pan and roast at 375 degrees for 15 to 17 minutes or to 150 degrees internally for medium-well.

Let stand for 3 to 5 minutes. Top each chop with about 2 1/2 ounces Apple Verjus and garnish with pepper and additional fresh herbs. Serve with herb-roasted potatoes and seasonal vegetables.

Serves 4

Apple Verjus

1 quart homemade or canned
    low-sodium chicken stock
1/2 cup fresh or frozen apple
    juice concentrate
1/3 cup packed brown sugar
1/4 cup chopped yellow onion
1 cinnamon stick
1/2 teaspoon red pepper flakes
salt and freshly ground pepper
    to taste
1 tablespoon cornstarch (optional)
1 tablespoon cold water (optional)

Combine the chicken stock, apple juice concentrate, brown sugar, onion, cinnamon stick and red pepper flakes in a heavy stockpot and mix well. Bring to a boil and reduce the heat. Simmer until reduced to about 2 1/2 cups. Season with salt and pepper and discard the cinnamon stick.

Thicken the mixture if necessary for the desired consistency. Blend the cornstarch and water in a cup and stir into the sauce. Simmer for 3 to 4 minutes, stirring constantly.

Makes 2 1/2 cups

Aloha Barbecue

THANKS TO THE CLEVER CLEAVER BROTHERS

1 (20-ounce) can juice-pack pineapple chunks
18 (1-inch) pieces red bell pepper
6 (1-inch) pieces pork tenderloin
6 (1-inch) pieces chicken tenders
6 large shrimp, peeled, deveined and butterflied
Wiki Sauce (below)

Soak eighteen (4-inch) wooden skewers in water in a bowl. Drain the pineapple, reserving the juice. Drain the skewers and thread one piece of bell pepper, one pineapple chunk and one piece of pork on each of six skewers. Thread one piece of bell pepper, one pineapple chunk and one piece of chicken on each of six skewers.

Thread just the tail of each shrimp on each of six skewers. Thread one piece of bell pepper and one pineapple chunk on each skewer and then thread the other end of the shrimp so it wraps around the bell pepper and pineapple. Combine with the reserved pineapple juice in a plastic container. Chill all the skewers, covered, in the refrigerator. Heat a grill to medium. Grill the skewers for about 2 minutes on each side or until cooked through. Remove to a platter and drizzle some of the Wiki Sauce over the pork, chicken and shrimp. Spoon the remaining Wiki Sauce into a bowl for dipping.

Makes 18

Wiki Sauce

THANKS TO THE CLEVER CLEAVER BROTHERS

3 garlic cloves, minced
1/2 cup chopped fresh cilantro
1 teaspoon hot sauce
juice of 1 lemon
1/4 teaspoon salt
1/8 teaspoon pepper
1/2 cup olive oil
1/2 cup crushed macadamias
1/4 cup (1 ounce) grated Parmesan cheese

Process the garlic, cilantro, hot sauce, lemon juice, salt and pepper in a blender for 10 seconds. Add the olive oil gradually, processing constantly. Add the macadamias and Parmesan cheese and process until smooth.

This recipe was tested with Cholula hot sauce.

Makes 1 3/4 cups

Cannellini Beans and Sausage

THANKS TO DOMINIC'S

1   pound Italian sausage,
    casings removed and
    sausage cut into quarters
1/4 cup olive oil
1   small onion, chopped
1   fresh tomato, peeled
    and chopped
3   garlic cloves, chopped
6   basil leaves
1   (15-ounce) can cannellini beans
1/2 cup dry white wine
4   ounces escarole, chopped
1   cup beef bouillon
salt and freshly ground pepper
    to taste

Cook the sausage with enough water to cover in a saucepan for 2 minutes; drain. Heat the olive oil in a large skillet and add the onion, tomato, garlic and basil. Sauté for 5 minutes. Add the sausage and beans and cook for 5 minutes. Add the white wine and simmer for 2 minutes. Stir in the escarole and beef bouillon and simmer for 10 minutes longer. Season with salt and pepper. Serve with toasted garlic cheese bread.

Serves 4

Dining In

Jambalaya

2   onions, chopped
4   green bell peppers, chopped
6   ribs celery, chopped
6   ounces sugar
8   ounces blackened seasoning
2   pounds margarine
4   cups cubed ham
4   cups chopped sausage
4   cups chopped chicken
1 1/2 quarts hot water
6 1/2 (16-ounce) cans diced tomatoes
7   (8-ounce) cans tomato sauce
4   bowls rice
3   tablespoons beef base

Combine the onions, bell peppers, celery, sugar and blackened seasoning with the margarine in a 6-inch saucepan. Cook over low heat until the margarine has melted.

Cook the ham, sausage and chicken in a large saucepan until brown. Add the hot water, tomatoes, tomato sauce, vegetables, rice and beef base; mix well. Cook, covered, for 25 minutes or until the rice is tender, stirring 4 or 5 times.

Serves 16

Heidi Glaus started out as an intern on the show,
and has held four different positions on the program:
intern, producer, reporter, and host.

Chicken Cacciatore

1 (3- to 3$\frac{1}{2}$-pound) chicken,
    cut up
all-purpose flour for dredging
salt and freshly ground pepper
    to taste
3 tablespoons extra-virgin olive oil
1 cup minced onion
$\frac{1}{2}$ cup chopped celery
8 ounces mushrooms, sliced
1$\frac{1}{2}$ teaspoons chopped fresh
    rosemary, or $\frac{1}{2}$ teaspoon
    dried rosemary
crushed red pepper flakes to taste
$\frac{1}{4}$ cup dry red wine
3 cups marinara sauce

Add the chicken to a mixture of flour, salt and pepper in a 1-gallon plastic bag. Shake to coat evenly and shake off any excess. Heat the olive oil in a large skillet over medium-high heat. Add the chicken, skin side down, in two batches and cook for 5 minutes on each side or until golden brown. Remove the chicken to a plate.

Add the onion, celery and mushrooms to the drippings in the skillet and sauté over medium heat for 8 to 10 minutes or until the onion is very tender. Add the rosemary, red pepper flakes, wine and marinara sauce and mix well.

Bring the sauce to a boil and return the chicken to the skillet. Bring to a boil and reduce the heat. Simmer for 20 to 25 minutes or until the chicken is cooked through and the juices run clear. Serve immediately.

Serves 4

Main Dishes

Barbecued Chicken Packet Dinner

THANKS TO THE ST. LOUIS DAIRY COUNCIL

3 tablespoons barbecue sauce
4 small boneless skinless chicken breasts
2 small red potatoes with skins, thinly sliced
1 red or green bell pepper, sliced
1 green onion, chopped
1/4 teaspoon salt
1/8 teaspoon pepper
1 1/2 cups (6 ounces) shredded Cheddar cheese

Place four 12×12-inch squares of foil on a work surface. Spread about 1 teaspoon of the barbecue sauce in the center of each foil sheet. Place one chicken breast on the barbecue sauce and spread about 1 teaspoon sauce over each piece. Top with the potato slices, bell pepper slices and green onion. Sprinkle with salt and pepper.

Fold the foil to enclose the chicken securely, sealing all the edges. Place on a baking sheet and bake at 375 degrees for 35 minutes. Open the packets with scissors and pull back the edges carefully, as the contents will be very hot and steam will escape. Sprinkle the Cheddar cheese evenly over the contents of the packets. Bake, unsealed, for 2 minutes longer, or until the cheese melts. Serve from the packets or remove to serving plates with a spatula if preferred.

Serves 4

Breast of Chicken with Balsamic Vinegar

THANKS TO DOMINIC'S

4   boneless skinless
     chicken breasts
salt and pepper to taste
all-purpose flour for coating
3   tablespoons olive oil
3   tablespoons unsalted butter
6   small shallots, chopped
2   garlic cloves, minced
1   bell pepper, seeded
     and chopped
3/4 cup red wine
6   tablespoons balsamic vinegar
2   cups chicken bouillon
5   fresh sage leaves, chopped
8   fresh parsley leaves, chopped

Season the chicken on both sides with salt and pepper and coat with flour. Heat the olive oil and butter in a skillet and add the chicken. Sauté until the chicken is light brown on both sides. Add the shallots, garlic and bell pepper and sauté for 2 to 3 minutes.

Stir in the wine and vinegar and cook for 1 minute. Add the chicken bouillon and sage. Cook for 8 to 10 minutes or until the chicken is tender. Remove the chicken to a warm plate. Cook the sauce until slightly thickened. Spoon over the chicken and sprinkle with the parsley.

Serves 4

Dining In

Main Dishes

Breast of Chicken Maria

2 cups chicken stock
1/3 cup sherry
1 teaspoon lemon juice
1/4 teaspoon minced garlic
1/2 cup (1 stick) butter
1/2 cup all-purpose flour
8 ounces lump crab meat
2 cups (8 ounces) shredded
   white American cheese
8 ounces mushrooms, sliced
1/2 teaspoon cracked pepper
4 (6-ounce) boneless skinless
   chicken breasts
salt and pepper to taste
flour for coating
vegetable oil for sautéing
12 asparagus spears, cooked

Combine the chicken stock, wine, lemon juice and garlic in a saucepan and bring to a boil. Reduce the heat and maintain at a simmer. Melt the butter in a medium saucepan and stir in 1/2 cup flour. Cook until light brown, stirring constantly. Add to the stock mixture and cook until smooth, stirring constantly. Reduce the heat to low and add the crab meat, cheese, mushrooms and 1/2 teaspoon cracked pepper. Keep warm.

Season the chicken with salt and pepper to taste and coat with additional flour. Sauté in a small amount of vegetable oil in a skillet until cooked through. Arrange the chicken on a serving platter and place three asparagus spears on each piece. Spoon the sauce over the top.

Serves 4

Chicken Breast Sorrentino

THANKS TO DOMINIC'S

4   boneless skinless
      chicken breasts
4   thin slices prosciutto
1/2   cup all-purpose flour
5   tablespoons olive oil
1   small onion, chopped
5   tablespoons olive oil
1   tomato, chopped
2   garlic cloves, chopped
6   tablespoons dry white wine
2   tablespoons unsalted butter
1   cup chicken stock
6   fresh basil leaves, chopped
salt and red pepper flakes to taste
1/4   cup (1 ounce) grated
      Parmesan cheese
4   ounces fresh buffalo mozzarella
      cheese, sliced
chopped parsley for garnish

   Pound the chicken breasts until thin on a work surface with a meat mallet. Layer the prosciutto over the chicken and coat lightly with the flour. Sauté the chicken in 5 tablespoons olive oil in a medium sauté pan until golden brown on all sides. Remove to a baking dish.
   Sauté the onion in 5 tablespoons olive oil in a medium skillet until translucent. Add the tomato and garlic and sauté for 5 minutes. Stir in the wine and simmer for several minutes. Add the butter, chicken stock, basil, salt and red pepper flakes and cook until reduced and thickened, stirring occasionally.
   Pour the sauce over the chicken. Sprinkle with the Parmesan cheese. Top with the mozzarella cheese. Broil until the cheese melts and the chicken is cooked through. Garnish with parsley.

   Serves 4

Chicken Pasta Peroni

THANKS TO DEL PIETRO'S

16 ounces bow tie pasta
2 (8-ounce) boneless skinless chicken breasts
2 tablespoons olive oil
1 tablespoon chopped garlic
1 each yellow and red bell peppers, sliced
2 cups chopped tomatoes
1 cup sliced mushrooms
salt, black pepper and red pepper flakes to taste
grated Parmesan cheese to taste

Cook the pasta using the package directions; drain and rinse. Grill the chicken until cooked through and cut into 1/2-inch strips.

Heat the olive oil in a very large skillet and add the garlic. Sauté for several minutes. Add the bell peppers and sauté just until tender-crisp. Add the chicken, tomatoes and mushrooms. Simmer for 5 minutes. Season with salt, black pepper and red pepper flakes. Add the pasta and toss to coat evenly. Top with Parmesan cheese.

Serves 4

Quick–and–Easy Tarragon Chicken

THANKS TO HEIDI GLAUS

2 tablespoons butter or margarine
1 tablespoon vegetable oil
4 boneless skinless chicken breasts
3/4 cup dry white wine or vermouth
2 teaspoons Dijon mustard
1 tablespoon chopped fresh tarragon, or 1 teaspoon dried tarragon
1/2 teaspoon salt
freshly ground pepper to taste
3/4 cup heavy cream

Heat the butter with the oil in a large skillet over medium heat. Add the chicken and cook for 4 minutes on each side. Remove to a plate.

Add the wine to the skillet and bring to a boil, stirring with a wooden spoon to deglaze the skillet. Stir in the Dijon mustard, tarragon, salt and pepper. Whisk in the cream and cook for 3 minutes or until slightly thickened.

Return the chicken to the skillet and turn to coat well. Simmer for 5 to 10 minutes or until the chicken is tender and cooked through. Remove the chicken to a serving plate and spoon the sauce over the top.

Serves 4

Chicken Spiedini with Portobello Mushrooms

THANKS TO DEL PIETRO'S

1/2 cup Del Pietro's salad dressing
juice of 1/2 lemon
splash of white wine
2   boneless skinless
    chicken breasts
1   cup bread crumbs
1/4 cup (1 ounce) grated
    Parmesan cheese
2   tablespoons chopped fresh
    Italian parsley
1/2 teaspoon minced garlic
salt and freshly ground pepper
    to taste
2   portobello mushrooms
extra-virgin olive oil for brushing
balsamic vinegar

Combine the salad dressing, lemon juice and wine in a bowl. Add the chicken and marinate in the refrigerator for 1 hour.

Mix the bread crumbs, Parmesan cheese, parsley, garlic, salt and pepper on a plate. Coat the chicken with the bread crumb mixture and thread onto skewers. Grill over medium-high heat for 10 minutes, turning to prevent burning the coating.

Brush the mushrooms with olive oil and season with salt and pepper. Bake or broil in a medium oven for about 3 minutes or until tender.

Remove the chicken from the skewers and arrange on serving plates with the mushrooms. Top with a dash of balsamic vinegar.

Serves 2

Dining In

Stuffed Chicken Breast

2   carrots, chopped
2   ribs celery, chopped
2   zucchini, chopped
1   cup bread crumbs
2   teaspoons minced garlic
1   teaspoon salt
2   teaspoons pepper
1/2 cup white wine
1   (8-ounce) whole chicken breast
Lemon Butter Sauce (below)

Combine the carrots, celery and zucchini in a large mixing bowl. Add the bread crumbs, garlic, salt and pepper. Stir in the wine.

Spread the vegetable mixture on the chicken and roll to enclose the filling; secure with a skewer. Place in a roasting pan and roast at 400 degrees for 18 to 22 minutes or until cooked through. Place on a serving plate and drizzle immediately with Lemon Butter Sauce.

Serves 1

Lemon Butter Sauce

1/2 cup (1 stick) unsalted butter
juice of 2 lemons, or 6 tablespoons
    lemon juice
1/2 cup white wine
3   tablespoons cornstarch
    (optional)
3   tablespoons water (optional)

Mix the butter, lemon juice and wine in a saucepan. Cook until the butter melts and the mixture is heated through. You can thicken the sauce with cornstarch or thin with water as needed for the desired consistency.

Makes 1 1/4 cups

Easy Chicken Enchiladas with Yogurt Sauce

THANKS TO THE ST. LOUIS DAIRY COUNCIL

2 cups plain low-fat yogurt
1 cup chopped cilantro
1 teaspoon ground cumin
3 ounces cream cheese
2 cups chopped cooked chicken breast
12 ounces chunky salsa
1/2 cup (2 ounces) shredded Mexican blend cheese
8 (6-inch) flour tortillas
1/2 cup (2 ounces) shredded Mexican blend cheese

Mix the yogurt, cilantro and cumin in a small bowl. Store in the refrigerator until needed.

Melt the cream cheese in a large skillet over medium heat. Add the chicken and 1/2 cup of the salsa and mix well. Stir in 1/2 cup cheese and cook until the cheese melts, stirring constantly. Spoon 1/3 cup of the chicken mixture onto each tortilla and roll the tortillas to enclose the filling. Place seam side down in an 8×12-inch baking dish. Sprinkle with the remaining salsa and 1/2 cup cheese.

Bake at 350 degrees for 15 minutes or until heated through. Serve with the yogurt sauce.

Serves 8

Kenny Rogers appeared on *Show Me St. Louis* in 1999.

Chicken Risotto with Asparagus

THANKS TO DOMINIC'S

8	ounces fresh asparagus, peeled and chopped
6	cups chicken stock
1	generous pinch saffron
1	small onion, finely chopped
3	tablespoons butter
2	cups arborio rice
1	small boneless skinless chicken breast, chopped
2/3	cup dry white wine
3	tablespoons butter
3/4	cup (3 ounces) freshly grated Parmesan cheese
salt and freshly ground pepper to taste	
2	tablespoon chopped fresh parsley

Blanch the asparagus in a medium saucepan of boiling water for 5 minutes. Remove the asparagus with a slotted spoon and reserve the cooking liquid. Combine 4 cups of the cooking liquid with the chicken stock and saffron in a saucepan. Bring to a simmer and keep hot.

Sauté the onion in 3 tablespoons butter in a large heavy saucepan until golden brown. Add the rice and sauté until well coated, stirring constantly. Stir in the asparagus and chicken. Cook for 2 to 3 minutes. Stir in the wine and cook for 2 minutes.

Add the hot liquid to the rice about $1/2$ cup at a time, cooking until the liquid has been absorbed after each addition and stirring constantly. Remove from the heat and stir in 3 tablespoons butter and the Parmesan cheese. Season with salt and pepper and sprinkle with the parsley. Serve immediately.

Serves 4

Stuffed Quail

2 tablespoons butter or margarine
1 pear, cored and chopped
1/2 small red onion, chopped
1 teaspoon fresh thyme
leaves, chopped
1 cup white wine
2 tablespoons chopped walnuts
2 tablespoons sun-dried raisins
salt and pepper to taste
1 tablespoon brown sugar
1 tablespoon chopped parsley
4 quail

Melt the butter in a skillet and add the pear, onion and thyme. Sauté for 4 to 5 minutes. Add the wine, walnuts, raisins, salt and pepper. Cook until the wine has evaporated. Stir in the brown sugar and parsley. Remove from the heat and spoon into a bowl. Chill in the refrigerator.

Spoon the mixture evenly into the cavities of each quail. Cross the quail legs and secure with a wooden pick. Place in a roasting pan and roast at 350 degrees for 30 minutes.

Serves 4

Dining In

Almond-Crusted Fresh Fish

THANKS TO BAHAMA BREEZE

1   slice fresh white bread
1/4 cup honey-roasted
    sliced almonds
1   teaspoon chopped fresh parsley
2   tablespoons butter, melted
1   teaspoon fresh lemon juice
4   (4-ounce) fresh fish fillets,
    1/2 inch thick
salt and pepper to taste
2   tablespoons olive oil
Lemon Butter Sauce (below)

Pulse the bread to crumbs in a food processor or blender. Sprinkle the crumbs on a baking sheet and toast at 350 degrees for 4 to 5 minutes or until light brown. Measure 1/4 cup of the crumbs and freeze the remaining crumbs for another use. Combine the crumbs with the almonds, parsley, butter and lemon juice in a microwave-safe bowl and mix well.

Season the fish on both sides with salt and pepper. Heat a 10-inch sauté pan over medium-high heat and add the olive oil and fish. Reduce the heat to medium and sauté the fish for 2 to 3 minutes on each side or just until it flakes easily. Place on a serving plate. Warm the almond mixture in the microwave for 30 seconds. Press over the fish and serve with warm Lemon Butter Sauce.

Serves 2

Lemon Butter Sauce

THANKS TO BAHAMA BREEZE

1   teaspoon chopped garlic
1   tablespoon olive oil
2   tablespoons white wine
1/2 teaspoon chopped fresh thyme
1   cup heavy cream
1   tablespoon fresh lemon juice
3   saffron threads
2   tablespoons butter, chilled
    and cubed
1   teaspoon cornstarch
1   teaspoon cold water
salt and white pepper to taste

Sauté the garlic in the olive oil in a heated small saucepan for 30 seconds. Add the wine and thyme and cook until reduced by one-half. Stir in the cream, lemon juice and saffron. Bring to a boil and reduce the heat to low. Add the butter and cook until the butter melts, stirring constantly to mix well.

Blend the cornstarch and water in a small bowl. Add to the hot mixture gradually and cook until thickened, stirring constantly. Season with salt and white pepper. Strain through a fine mesh sieve and serve hot.

Makes 1 1/2 cups

Salmon with Linguini and Pesto Sauce

THANKS TO DOMINIC'S

3/4 cup fresh basil leaves
3 or 4 garlic cloves
3 tablespoons pine nuts
3 tablespoons olive oil
1 large tomato, chopped
1/2 teaspoon salt
freshly ground pepper to taste
16 ounces linguini
8 ounces fresh salmon,
    coarsely chopped
2 tablespoons olive oil
1/2 cup (2 ounces) grated
    pecorino cheese

Combine the basil, garlic, pine nuts, 3 tablespoons olive oil, the tomato, salt and pepper in a food processor and process until smooth. Cook the pasta al dente in salted water using the package directions. Drain, reserving 1/4 cup of the cooking liquid. Add the reserved cooking liquid to the pesto mixture and process until smooth.

Sauté the salmon in 2 tablespoons olive oil in a skillet for 4 minutes. Combine with the pasta and pesto sauce in a bowl and toss gently to mix well. Serve immediately with the pecorino cheese.

Serves 4

Captain Kangaroo appeared on
Show Me St. Louis in 1996.

Main Dishes

Steamed Salmon with Ponzu Sauce

THANKS TO MIKE SHANNON'S RESTAURANT

4   (8-ounce) fresh Atlantic
    salmon fillets
2   carrots, thickly sliced
2   zucchini, thickly sliced
2   yellow squash, thickly sliced
1   head broccoli, cut into florets
12 button mushrooms
1   (7- to 8-ounce) package
    Japanese noodles
Ponzu Sauce (below)

Combine the salmon, carrots, zucchini, yellow squash, broccoli, mushrooms and noodles in a bamboo steamer or large saucepan fitted with a steamer insert. Steam over boiling water for 10 to 15 minutes or until the salmon and vegetables are tender. Spoon onto 4 serving plates and top each serving with 1 to 2 tablespoons Ponzu Sauce.

Yakisoba and other precooked Japanese noodles are available in the produce section of many supermarkets. You can use uncooked noodles and follow the package directions for four servings. Add to the steamed salmon and vegetables.

Serves 4

Ponzu Sauce

THANKS TO MIKE SHANNON'S RESTAURANT

3/4 cup soy sauce
1/4 cup fresh lemon juice
3   tablespoons rice vinegar or
     white vinegar
3   tablespoons sugar
1   tablespoon minced green onions
1/2 teaspoon minced or
     shredded fresh ginger

Combine the soy sauce, lemon juice, vinegar and sugar in a bowl and mix to dissolve the sugar. Add the green onions and ginger and mix well. Store in the refrigerator if not used immediately.

Makes 1 1/2 cups

Salmon Picante

THANKS TO DOMINIC'S

1/4 cup olive oil
1 large shallot, chopped
2 garlic cloves, finely chopped
1/4 cup dry white wine
1 ounce pimento, chopped
2 ounces capers
1 cup fish stock
1 cup heavy cream
juice of 1/2 lemon
1/4 cup (1/2 stick) unsalted butter
salt and pepper to taste
2 pounds fresh salmon
olive oil for drizzling
chopped parsley for garnish

Heat 1/4 cup olive oil in a medium skillet and add the shallot and garlic. Sauté for 3 minutes. Stir in the wine, pimento and capers. Cook for 3 minutes. Add the fish stock, cream, lemon juice, butter, salt and pepper. Remove from the heat and let stand to thicken.

Season the salmon lightly with salt and pepper. Drizzle with additional olive oil. Grill for 10 minutes or until the fish flakes easily. Remove to a platter and drizzle with the sauce. Garnish with parsley.

Serves 4

Dining In

Dining In

Roasted Tilapia on Spinach
with Lemon Vinaigrette

extra-virgin olive oil
kosher salt and cracked pepper
    to taste
2 (16-ounce) packages
    fresh spinach
4 (6-ounce) tilapia fillets
2 tablespoons butter
juice of 3 lemons
freshly ground pepper to taste

Heat a small amount of olive oil in a large ovenproof sauté pan. Sprinkle kosher salt and cracked pepper in the hot oil. Add the spinach and sauté until the spinach is tender. Remove the spinach to a plate and cool to room temperature.

Season the fish with kosher salt and cracked pepper. Place the sauté pan back on the heat and arrange the fish round side down in the pan. Cook for 1 minute. Add the butter and place the pan in a 375-degree oven. Bake for 4 to 5 minutes or until the fish is cooked through. Cool slightly.

Spoon the spinach onto serving plates and place the fish over the spinach. Add the lemon juice and an equal amount of olive oil to the sauté pan and mix well. Season with kosher salt and ground pepper and drizzle over the fish and around the plates.

Serves 4

In the beginning of the show, all of the stories were viedotaped, edited, and reported in the same day. Today, stories are typically shot the day before they air.

Fettucini with Lobster

THANKS TO DOMINIC'S

3   tablespoons olive oil
1/2 onion, finely chopped
1   large tomato, peeled
    and chopped
2   garlic cloves, finely chopped
1/2 cup dry sherry
12 ounces lobster meat
1/2 cup heavy cream
5   tablespoons butter
16 ounces fettucini
salt to taste
2/3 cup grated Parmesan cheese
3   tablespoons finely
    chopped parsley
freshly ground pepper to taste

Heat the olive oil in a large skillet and add the onion, tomato and garlic. Cook for 10 minutes, stirring frequently. Add the wine and simmer for 5 minutes. Stir in the lobster, cream and butter and cook for 5 minutes.

Cook the pasta in boiling salted water in a large saucepan for 8 to 10 minutes or until al dente; drain. Mix with the sauce, Parmesan cheese and parsley in the saucepan. Season with salt and pepper and toss to mix well. Cook just until heated through and creamy. Serve immediately.

You can add warm water if needed for the desired consistency.

Serves 4

Main Dishes

Lobster and
Mushroom Risotto

5   cups lobster stock or
     chicken stock
2   tablespoons butter
1   tablespoon olive oil
2   tablespoons chopped onion
1   tablespoon chopped shallot
1   teaspoon minced garlic
1   cup sliced mixture of shiitake
     and portobello mushroom caps
salt and pepper to taste
1 1/2 cups arborio rice
1/2 cup white vermouth
1   tablespoon finely chopped
     peeled carrots
1   tablespoon finely chopped
     peeled zucchini
1/2 teaspoon fish sauce,
     or to taste
8   ounces cooked lobster meat,
     chopped
2   tablespoons chopped chives
1   teaspoon truffle oil

Bring the lobster stock to a simmer in a large saucepan and maintain the temperature of the stock.

Heat the butter with the olive oil in a large saucepan over low heat. Add the onion and shallot and sauté for 1 minute or until translucent. Add the garlic and sauté for 1 minute. Add the mushrooms, salt and pepper and increase the heat. Cook until the mushrooms have cooked down. Stir in the rice. Sauté for 1 to 2 minutes longer or until the rice is light brown.

Add the wine and cook until the wine is absorbed, stirring constantly. Add the carrots and zucchini. Add the hot lobster stock 1 1/2 cups at a time and cook until the liquid is fully absorbed after each addition, stirring constantly; the process should require about 10 minutes. Season with the fish sauce and fold in the lobster and chives. Add the truffle oil just before serving. Spoon into heated bowls. Serve immediately.

This recipe was tested with Martini & Rossi white vermouth.

Serves 2

Lobster Rockefeller
à la Faust's

THANKS TO THE ADAM'S MARK HOTEL

1 (1 1/2-pound) lobster
2 tablespoons finely chopped shallots
1 tablespoon butter, melted
3 ounces fresh spinach
3 tablespoons Pernod
2 tablespoons sherry
2 tablespoons heavy cream
salt and white pepper to taste

Cook the lobster in enough water to cover in a large saucepan for 9 to 12 minutes or until cooked through; drain. Plunge into ice water to cool. Remove the meat from the tail, reserving the shell, and slice the meat. Remove the meat from the claws and reserve for the garnish.

Sauté the shallots in the butter in a saucepan over medium heat for 2 to 3 minutes. Add the spinach and sauté for 1 to 2 minutes or until tender. Remove from the heat and stir in the liqueur and wine. Increase the heat to high and return the saucepan to the heat.

Ignite the mixture carefully and allow the flames to subside. Stir in the cream and bring to a boil. Reduce the heat and cook until the mixture thickens, stirring frequently. Season with salt and white pepper.

Add the lobster tail meat to the sauce and heat to serving temperature. Spoon the mixture into the reserve lobster tail shell and garnish with the claw meat.

Serves 2

Lobster and Shrimp Pasta

THANKS TO BAHAMA BREEZE

2   (5- to 6-ounce) lobster tails
10   ounces medium shrimp
salt and pepper to taste
8   ounces pasta
2   tablespoons olive oil
4   ounces mushrooms, sliced
2   tablespoons Brandy Cream
    Sauce (below)
2   green onions, thinly sliced
1   tablespoons finely chopped
    fresh parsley

Cut the lobster tails into halves with kitchen shears and remove the meat from the tails. Cut the lobster meat into 1/2-inch pieces. Peel the shrimp. Reserve the lobster and shrimp shells for the Brandy Cream Sauce. Season the lobster and shrimp with salt and pepper and chill.

Cook the pasta using the package directions; drain and rinse with cold water. Heat the olive oil in a large nonstick skillet over high heat. Add the lobster, shrimp and mushrooms. Sauté for 2 to 3 minutes or until the lobster and shrimp are opaque.

Reduce the heat to medium and add the Brandy Cream Sauce and green onions. Bring to a boil, stirring constantly. Add the pasta and cook until heated through, adding cream or milk if needed for the desired consistency. Serve hot and top with the parsley.

Serves 2

Brandy Cream Sauce

THANKS TO BAHAMA BREEZE

1 1/4 teaspoons cornstarch
2   teaspoons cool water
1/4   cup white wine
4   saffron threads
1   teaspoon dried basil
1/2   teaspoon dried thyme
reserved lobster and shrimp shells
1/2   cup chicken broth
1   cup heavy cream
salt and white pepper to taste
2   tablespoons brandy

Blend the cornstarch and water in a small cup and set aside. Combine the wine, saffron, basil, thyme and reserved lobster and shrimp shells in a 1-quart saucepan. Bring to a boil and reduce the heat. Simmer until the liquid is reduced by one-half. Add the chicken broth and cream and return to a boil over medium heat.

Whisk in the cornstarch mixture gradually and reduce the heat to low. Simmer for 2 to 3 minutes, stirring frequently. Season with salt and white pepper. Remove from the heat and stir in the brandy. Strain through a fine mesh strainer.

Makes 1 1/2 cups

Mussels Pomodoro

1/4 cup chopped fresh basil
6 to 8 garlic cloves, chopped
1 1/4 cups chopped Roma tomatoes
1/4 teaspoon crushed red
    pepper flakes
1/8 teaspoon coarsely ground
    black pepper
olive oil for sautéing
3/4 cup chianti
1 cup clam juice
3 cups marinara sauce
3 pounds mussels
cooked linguini

Sauté the basil, garlic, tomatoes, red pepper flakes and black pepper in a small amount of olive oil in a skillet. Add the wine, stirring to deglaze the skillet. Stir in the clam juice, marinara sauce and mussels. Bring to a simmer and simmer for 10 minutes. Toss with the linguini in a bowl and serve immediately.

You can omit the linguini to serve this dish as an appetizer.

Serves 4

Linguini Tutto Mare

THANKS TO DEL PIETRO'S

4 ounces linguini
salt to taste
1 1/2 cups half-and-half
3 ounces small shrimp, peeled
    and deveined, about 1/2 cup
5 ounces sea scallops, about 5
4 ounces canned chopped clams,
    drained, about 1/2 cup
3/4 teaspoon chopped garlic
1 1/2 teaspoons butter
1/8 teaspoon red pepper flakes
freshly ground black pepper to taste
1/2 cup (2 ounces) grated
    Parmesan cheese

Cook the pasta in salted water in a saucepan using the package directions; drain. Bring the half-and-half to a boil in a large skillet over medium heat. Cook until reduced by one-fourth, stirring frequently.

Stir in the shrimp, scallops, clams, garlic, butter, red pepper flakes and black pepper. Cook for 5 minutes or until the scallops are opaque, stirring constantly. Stir in the Parmesan cheese and remove from the heat. Toss with the pasta in a bowl and serve immediately.

Serves 1

Main Dishes

Scallops and Pancetta with Capellini

THANKS TO THE KELLY TWINS

1   gallon water
salt to taste
6   ounces pancetta, cut into
     1/2 inch pieces or strips
1   pound sea scallops or bay
     scallops, trimmed
1/8 teaspoon red pepper flakes
freshly ground black pepper to taste
1   cup (1/2-inch) diagonally-
     cut leeks
2   tablespoons (or more)
     minced garlic
3/4 cup white wine
16   ounces capellini
1   head radicchio or escarole or a
     mixture, cut chiffanade
2   tablespoons finely chopped
     Italian parsley
2   tablespoons finely chopped basil
chopped tomatoes, cherry tomatoes,
     grape tomatoes or pear
     tomatoes (optional)

Bring the water to a boil in a large saucepan and add salt to taste.

Cook the pancetta in a large sauté pan over medium heat until it begins to crisp. Remove to a bowl with a slotted spoon. Increase the heat to high and add the scallops. Season with salt, red pepper flakes and black pepper. Cook until light brown and springy to the touch; sea scallops will take a minute longer than bay scallops, but do not overcook. Remove with a slotted spoon to the bowl with the pancetta.

Pour any excess drippings from the sauté pan, leaving just enough to coat the pan. Reduce the heat to medium and add the leeks. Sauté for 5 minutes. Add the garlic and sauté just until the garlic is aromatic. Stir in the wine and cook until the wine is reduced by one-half.

Add the pasta to the saucepan of boiling water and cook for just 3 minutes or until al dente. Drain, reserving 1/2 cup of the cooking liquid; do not rinse.

Add the radicchio to the leek mixture in the sauté pan and return the scallops and pancetta with any accumulated juices to the pan. Add the pasta, parsley, basil and tomatoes and toss to mix well. Add enough of the reserved cooking liquid to make the desired consistency. Adjust the salt and serve.

Serves 4

Brentwood Pasta

THANKS TO J. BUCKS

5 shrimp, peeled, deveined
   and chopped
2 ounces andouille sausage, sliced
olive oil for sautéing
1 teaspoon chopped garlic
1 cup Spicy Cream (below)
2 ounces roasted red
   pepper, chopped
12 ounces linguini, cooked
1 tablespoon chopped tomato
2 ounces grated Parmesan cheese

Sauté the shrimp and andouille sausage in a small amount of olive oil in a saucepan. Add the garlic and sauté for 1 minute. Stir in the Spicy Cream and roasted red pepper and cook until reduced by one-half. Add the linguini and toss to coat evenly. Top with the tomato and Parmesan cheese.

Serves 2

Spicy Cream

THANKS TO J. BUCKS

1 jalapeño chile,
   coarsely chopped
1/2 cup coarsely chopped onion
olive oil for sautéing
1 tablespoon chipotle purée
1 teaspoon ground cumin
1 teaspoon chili powder
1 quart 40% heavy cream
3 tablespoons roasted
   garlic purée

Sauté the jalapeño chile and onion in a small amount of olive oil in a saucepan. Add the chipotle purée, cumin and chili powder; mix well. Stir in the cream and garlic purée. Bring to a boil and reduce to a simmer. Cook for 10 minutes. Strain into a container and store in the refrigerator.

Makes 4 1/2 cups

Dining In

Shrimp alla Marinara

THANKS TO DOMINIC'S

1	pound shrimp, peeled and deveined
1	cup all-purpose flour
3	tablespoons olive oil
1/2	cup dry white wine
12	ounces chopped canned tomatoes
3	garlic cloves, chopped
6	pitted olives, chopped
1/2	cup sliced mushrooms
1/2	onion, chopped
1	ounce capers
1	tablespoon butter
salt to taste	
1/8	teaspoon red pepper
1/4	cup chopped fresh Italian parsley

Coat the shrimp lightly with the flour. Heat the olive oil in a large skillet and add the shrimp. Sauté for 3 minutes, turning to sauté both sides. Add the wine, tomatoes, garlic, olives, mushrooms, onion, capers, butter, salt and red pepper; mix well. Cook for 5 minutes. Remove the shrimp to a warm serving plate with a slotted spoon. Cook the sauce over medium heat for 10 minutes longer. Spoon over the shrimp and sprinkle with the parsley. Serve over toasted bread or pasta.

Serves 4

Shrimp and Mushrooms

24	(10- to 15-count) shrimp
1	tablespoon olive oil
1	cup white wine
1 1/2	cups 40% heavy cream
1	teaspoon chopped garlic
2	cups chopped mushrooms
1/2	teaspoon oregano
1	teaspoon feta cheese
1	teaspoon grated Parmesan cheese
juice of 2 lemons	
1	teaspoon chopped fresh parsley
salt and pepper to taste	

Sauté the shrimp in the olive oil in a saucepan for 30 seconds on each side; shrimp will be partially cooked and beginning to turn pink. Add the wine and cook until slightly reduced, stirring to deglaze the skillet. Add the cream, garlic and mushrooms. Cook until the mixture is reduced by almost one-half. Stir in the oregano. Add the feta cheese and Parmesan cheese and cook until the cheeses melt and the sauce is thickened to the desired consistency. Stir in the lemon juice, parsley, salt and pepper.

Serves 4

Barbecued Shrimp

THANKS TO THE ST. LOUIS STEAKHOUSE

6   (10-to 15-count) shrimp
1   tablespoon Cajun seasoning
2   tablespoons olive oil
1   tablespoon chopped garlic
1   tablespoon Worcestershire sauce
1   tablespoon smoked
    chipotle sauce
1   tablespoon lemon juice
1/4 cup chablis
1/4 cup heavy cream
1/4 cup chopped green onions
1   tablespoon butter

Season the shrimp with the Cajun seasoning. Heat the olive oil to smoking in a skillet. Add the shrimp and garlic and sauté for 1 minute. Add the Worcestershire sauce, chipotle sauce, lemon juice and wine. Cook until reduced by one-half. Stir in the cream and green onions and cook until reduced by one-half. Remove from the heat and stir in the butter.

This recipe was tested with Tabasco smoked chipotle sauce and Lea & Perrins Worcestershire sauce.

Serves 1

Scampi Italiana

THANKS TO DOMINIC'S

18 large shrimp, peeled
    and deveined
1/2 cup all-purpose flour
salt to taste
2   tablespoons olive oil
4   garlic cloves, chopped
1/2 cup dry white wine
1   cup fish stock
1/2 cup sliced mushrooms
juice of 1 lemon
2   tablespoons butter
pepper to taste
1/4 cup chopped fresh parsley

Coat the shrimp lightly with the flour and sprinkle with salt. Heat the olive oil in a large skillet over medium heat. Add the shrimp and sauté until golden brown on both sides. Add the garlic and wine. Simmer for 2 minutes. Add the fish stock, mushrooms, lemon juice and butter and simmer for 8 minutes or until the sauce thickens. Season with salt and pepper and sprinkle with the parsley.

Serves 3

Sides & Meatless Main Dishes

Bevo Mill

I have a family who is nice—fun but sometimes serious. I wanted a forever family that was nice and caring and helpful and fun and now I have that!

—Carrie, age 15, adopted

When children come into foster care, they lose connections with their past. Childhood mementos, such as baby photos, school pictures, or snapshots of grandma or siblings, are lost. Carrie's Little Wish was for a camera. Now that Carrie is adopted, she will begin building new childhood memories, one photo at a time.

Broccoli Cheddar Puff

THANKS TO THE MISSOURI EGG COUNCIL

5   tablespoons butter
6   tablespoons all-purpose flour
1/2 teaspoon salt
1/8 teaspoon cayenne pepper
2 1/4 cups milk
2   cups (8 ounces) shredded
     sharp Cheddar cheese
7   egg whites
7   egg yolks, beaten
2   (10-ounce) packages frozen
     broccoli, thawed and drained
1 1/2 cups coarsely crumbled soft
     bread, about 3 slices bread

Melt the butter in a medium saucepan. Stir in the flour, salt and cayenne pepper and cook until bubbly. Add the milk gradually and cook until thickened, stirring constantly. Add the cheese and cook until melted, stirring to blend evenly.

Beat the egg whites in a large mixing bowl until stiff but not dry. Stir a small amount of the hot cheese sauce into the egg yolks, and then stir the egg yolks into the cheese sauce. Add the broccoli. Fold in the egg whites gently. Spoon into a buttered 3 1/2-quart baking dish and top with the bread crumbs.

Bake at 325 degrees on the lowest oven rack for 40 minutes. Serve immediately.

Serves 8

The show first hit the air on September 5, 1995.

Eggplant Parmesan

THANKS TO DOMINIC'S

1/4 cup virgin olive oil
1 small red or yellow onion, minced
2 garlic cloves, minced
salt and pepper to taste
2 pounds ripe tomatoes, peeled, seeded and chopped
2 firm eggplant, about 2 pounds
2 quarts peanut oil or safflower oil
1 pound fresh whole-milk mozzarella cheese, thinly sliced
1 cup (4 ounces) grated Parmigiano–Reggiano cheese
1/2 cup loosely packed fresh basil leaves, sliced with scissors

Heat the olive oil in a large skillet over medium heat. Add the onion, garlic, salt and pepper and sauté for 3 to 4 minutes or until the onion is translucent. Add the tomatoes and simmer for 15 minutes or until the sauce begins to thicken.

Cut the unpeeled eggplant lengthwise into very thin slices. Heat the peanut oil to 360 degrees in a heavy 3-quart saucepan or deep fryer. Deep-fry the eggplant two or three slices at a time for 3 to 4 minutes or until golden brown. Remove to paper towels to drain and season with salt and pepper.

Spread several tablespoons of the tomato sauce in a 9×13-inch baking dish. Arrange one-third of the eggplant slices in the prepared dish. Spread one-third of the remaining tomato sauce over the slices and top with half the mozzarella cheese slices. Layer half the remaining eggplant slices, half the remaining sauce and half the Parmigiano-Reggiano cheese in the dish. Top with the remaining eggplant, sauce, mozzarella cheese and Parmigiano-Reggiano cheese. Sprinkle with the basil.

Bake at 400 degrees on the center rack in the oven for 40 minutes or until bubbly. Serve warm or at room temperature.

Serves 8

Sides & Meatless
Main Dishes

Mushroom Asparagus Wraps

THANKS TO THE KELLY TWINS

1/4 cup olive oil
12 ounces mushrooms, sliced
1 yellow onion, julienned
2 garlic cloves, minced
salt and pepper to taste
16 ounces asparagus, trimmed
and cut diagonally into
1/2-inch pieces
3 tablespoons (or less) chopped
fresh herbs, such as Italian
parsley, tarragon and/or chervil
6 (8-inch) flour tortillas, warmed
12 ounces White Bean Mash
(page 18), or hummus
6 ounces goat cheese

Heat the olive oil in a large heavy skillet over medium-high heat. Add the mushrooms, onion and garlic and sauté until the mushrooms are tender and begin to brown. Season with salt and pepper. Add the asparagus and cook, covered, for 1 minute longer. Sprinkle with the herbs and remove from the heat.

Spread each warmed tortilla with 1 to 2 ounces White Bean Mash. Top with a generous amount of the mushroom mixture. Crumble the goat cheese over the top. Roll the tortillas to enclose the filling and serve immediately.

You can be creative with the filling for this recipe, adding reconstituted sun-dried tomatoes, other cheeses, and/or sliced black olives. This was tested with Goatsbeard goat cheese, made in Missouri, and Ozark Mushroom Farms mushrooms.

Serves 6

Stuffed Mushrooms

1 cup fresh spinach
10 to 12 mushrooms
1 tablespoon minced garlic
1 tablespoon unsalted butter
1/4 teaspoon oregano
1 tablespoon lemon juice
2 eggs
2 tablespoons bread crumbs

Rinse the spinach and place while still damp in a medium ovenproof skillet sprayed with nonstick cooking spray. Sauté over medium heat for 2 minutes. Drain in a strainer, pressing to remove the moisture, and chop.

Remove the stems from the mushrooms and chop finely, reserving the caps. Sauté the garlic in the butter in a small skillet for 1 minute. Add the mushroom stems, spinach and oregano and sauté for 2 minutes. Stir in the lemon juice and remove from the heat.

Beat the eggs in a small bowl. Place the bread crumbs in a small bowl. Dip the mushroom caps in the beaten eggs one at a time and coat with the bread crumbs. Spoon the spinach mixture into the mushroom caps and arrange in a baking pan. Bake at 400 degrees for 12 minutes or until light brown.

You can also serve this as an appetizer.

Serves 5 to 6

Roasted Potatoes

8 ounces tiny red potatoes, cut into halves
3 garlic cloves
1 teaspoon olive oil
pepper to taste
1 teaspoon chopped chives

Arrange the potatoes in a single layer in a baking dish. Place the garlic cloves between the potatoes. Drizzle with the olive oil and sprinkle with pepper. Bake at 350 degrees for 30 to 40 minutes or until the potatoes and garlic are tender. Remove the garlic and squeeze over the potatoes. Sprinkle with the chives and additional pepper. Serve with beef or chicken.

Serves 2

Portobello Mushrooms Stuffed with Spinach and Sun-Dried Tomatoes

THANKS TO PORTABELLA'S

1/4 cup olive oil
1 garlic clove, minced
2 tablespoons balsamic vinegar
4 large portobello mushrooms caps
salt and pepper to taste
1/4 cup chopped onion
1 tablespoon olive oil
1 garlic clove, minced
8 sun-dried tomatoes, julienned
1/2 cup cream
10 ounces spinach
1/4 cup (1 ounce) shredded or grated asiago cheese
1 (4-ounce) ball fresh mozzarella cheese, chopped
2 tablespoons toasted bread crumbs

Mix 1/4 cup olive oil, 1 garlic clove and the vinegar in a bowl. Brush the mushrooms caps generously with the mixture and season with salt and pepper. Grill or roast in a hot oven until tender.

Sauté the onion in 1 tablespoon olive oil in a skillet. Add 1 garlic clove and the sun-dried tomatoes and sauté for 30 seconds. Add the cream and cook until reduced to the desired consistency. Stir in the spinach and cook until wilted; season with salt and pepper. Stir in the asiago cheese and mozzrella cheese and heat until the cheeses melt. Spoon into the mushroom caps and top with the toasted bread crumbs.

Serve as a side dish, with mixed greens as a warm salad or as an appetizer.

Serves 4

Spinach Cheese Bake

1 (10-ounce) package frozen
   chopped spinach
1 to 2 tablespoons
   all-purpose flour
2 eggs, beaten
3 ounces cream cheese, cubed
3/4 cup cubed American cheese
1/4 cup (1/2 stick) butter, cubed
1 1/2 teaspoons instant onion flakes
1/2 teaspoon salt
1/2 cup fine bread crumbs
1/4 cup (1/2 stick) butter
1/3 cup grated Parmesan cheese

Cook the spinach in a 1 1/2-quart saucepan using the package directions; remove from the heat and drain. Sprinkle the flour gradually over the spinach, stirring constantly to mix well. Add the eggs, cream cheese, American cheese, 1/4 cup butter, the onion flakes and salt; mix well. Cook until the cheeses melt, stirring constantly. Spoon into a baking dish.

Combine the bread crumbs and 1/4 cup butter in a small baking dish. Bake at 350 degrees until the butter melts and toss to mix well. Sprinkle over the spinach mixture and top with the Parmesan cheese. Bake for 30 minutes.

You may also prepare this in the microwave.

Serves 4

On average, eighty thousand viewers watch
Show Me St. Louis every day at 3 p.m.

Sides & Meatless
Main Dishes

Sweet Potato Soufflé

3   cups mashed cooked
    sweet potatoes
1/2 cup flaked coconut
1/2 cup raisins
1   cup sugar
1/2 cup milk
1/3 cup melted butter
2   eggs, beaten
1   teaspoon vanilla extract
Sweet Potato Topping (below)

Combine the sweet potatoes, coconut and raisins in a large bowl. Add the sugar, milk, butter, eggs and vanilla and mix well. Spoon into a greased baking dish. Sprinkle with Sweet Potato Topping and bake at 300 degrees until the topping is golden brown and the sweet potatoes are heated through.

Serves 8

Sweet Potato Topping

1   cup flaked coconut
1   cup chopped nuts
1   cup packed brown sugar
1/2 cup all-purpose flour
1/3 cup melted butter

Combine the coconut, nuts, brown sugar, flour and butter in a bowl and mix well.

Makes 3 1/2 cups

Bow Tie Pasta with Gorgonzola and Fresh Tomato Sauce

THANKS TO DOMINIC'S

3/4 cup (3 ounces) chopped
    gorgonzola cheese
1 cup half-and-half
1/2 small red onion, chopped
1 red bell pepper, grilled, peeled
    and chopped
3 garlic cloves, minced
3 tomatoes, peeled, seeded
    and chopped
5 tablespoons virgin olive oil
1/4 cup dry white wine
9 fresh basil leaves
salt and pepper to taste
16 ounces bow tie pasta
1/2 cup (2 ounces) grated
    Parmesan cheese

Combine the gorgonzola cheese and half-and-half in a medium saucepan over low heat. Cook until the cheese melts completely, stirring to blend well; remove from the heat.

Sauté the onion, bell pepper, garlic and tomatoes in the olive oil in a skillet for 8 to 10 minutes or until tender. Stir in the wine, basil, salt and pepper. Simmer for 6 minutes longer; remove from the heat.

Cook the pasta in boiling salted water in a saucepan for 7 minutes. Drain and return the pasta to the saucepan. Add the cheese mixture and toss to coat evenly. Add half the tomato sauce mixture and toss to mix. Spoon into pasta bowls and top evenly with the remaining tomato sauce mixture. Sprinkle with the Parmesan cheese and serve immediately.

Serves 4

Fresh Italian Pasta

THANKS TO HAUTLY CHEESE

8   ounces bow tie pasta
1   garlic clove, crushed
3   large tomatoes, chopped
1   (15-ounce) can Great Northern
    beans or other white beans,
    drained and rinsed
5   cups coarsely chopped
    fresh spinach
1/4 cup chicken broth
3/4 cup (3 ounces) grated Hautly
    Romano cheese
freshly ground pepper to taste

Cook the pasta using the package directions; drain and keep warm. Grease a nonstick skillet lightly and heat over medium-high heat. Sauté the garlic and tomatoes in the skillet for 2 minutes or until the tomatoes are partially tender.

Stir in the beans, spinach and chicken broth. Cook just until the spinach wilts, stirring constantly. Add the pasta to the spinach mixture. Stir in the Romano cheese and season with pepper. Toss lightly and serve immediately.

Serves 2

Rigatoni Amatriciana

THANKS TO DOMINIC'S

1   small onion, chopped
8   ounces pancetta, chopped
3   garlic cloves, chopped
6   tablespoons olive oil
3/4 cup dry white wine
1   (22-ounce) can peeled whole
    tomatoes, chopped
2   tablespoons unsalted butter
salt, red pepper and black pepper
    to taste
16 ounces rigatoni
1   cup (4 ounces) grated
    Parmesan cheese
chopped parsley to taste

Sauté the onion, pancetta and garlic in the hot olive oil in a large skillet for 7 minutes. Add the wine and cook for 2 minutes. Add the tomatoes, butter, salt, red pepper and black pepper. Cook for 15 minutes, stirring occasionally.

Cook the pasta in salted water in a medium saucepan for 8 minutes or until al dente. Drain and add the sauce and half the Parmesan cheese. Spoon onto a serving platter and sprinkle with parsley and the remaining Parmesan cheese.

Serves 4

Portobello Tortellini

5 ounces portobello mushrooms
or other mushrooms, sliced
cloves of 2 small bulbs roasted garlic
1/4 teaspoon kosher salt
1/4 teaspoon cracked black pepper
1/8 teaspoon crushed red
pepper flakes
2 teaspoons extra-virgin olive oil
2 tablespoons dry white wine
1/2 cup chopped tomato
1 quart water
1/4 teaspoon salt
12 ounces fresh tortellini filled with
wild mushrooms or cheese
grated asiago cheese for garnish

Sauté the mushrooms and garlic with the kosher salt, black pepper and red pepper flakes in the olive oil in a saucepan over high heat for 3 minutes. Stir in the wine and tomato. Cook for 2 minutes longer.

Bring the water and 1/4 teaspoon salt to a boil in a large saucepan. Add the pasta and cook for 4 minutes; drain. Add the mushroom mixture and toss to mix well. Garnish with asiago cheese and serve immediately.

You may substitute 15 garlic cloves sautéed in 1 teaspoon olive oil for 5 minutes for the roasted garlic if preferred.

Serves 4

The first week of the show never made
the air back in 1995. It was a dress rehearsal
for the thousands of shows to come.

Dining In

Spinach and Ricotta Ravioli

2   tablespoon extra-virgin olive oil
3   garlic cloves, minced
1   (10-ounce) package fresh
    spinach, stemmed
salt and freshly ground pepper
    to taste
7   to 8 ounces ricotta cheese
1   egg, lightly beaten
1/2 cup (2 ounces) grated
    pecorino-Romano cheese
1/8 teaspoon freshly grated nutmeg
8   ounces fresh basic pasta dough
1   tablespoon kosher salt
4   to 6 quarts water
Tomato Pancetta Butter and
    2 tablespoons reserved
    pancetta (page 101)
grated pecorino-Romano cheese
    and thyme sprigs for garnish

Heat the olive oil in a large heated sauté pan over medium heat. Add the garlic and sauté for 15 to 20 seconds or just until it begins to sizzle. Add the spinach in batches, sautéing for 3 minutes or until wilted and bright green after each addition. Season generously with salt and pepper. Remove to a parchment-lined tray to cool. Squeeze dry in a dampened cheesecloth.

Combine the spinach with the ricotta cheese, egg, pecorino-Romano cheese and nutmeg in a bowl. Season with salt and pepper and mix well.

Roll the pasta dough through a pasta machine, starting at the #1 setting and ending with the #6 setting; you will need 2 sheets of the pasta dough. Place 1 sheet on a work surface and dollop the spinach mixture onto the pasta in rows, using 2 tablespoonfuls at a time; leave a 3/4-inch border around the edges and 2 inches between the dollops. Moisten the border and between the filling with water. Place the second sheet of pasta on top and press firmly around the edges and between the filling. Cut into squares with a pastry cutter. Remove to a tray or kitchen towel dusted with flour; let stand for 5 to 10 minutes to dry.

Bring the water and kosher salt to a boil in an 8-quart saucepan. Cook the pasta in the boiling water for 2 minutes or until al dente and floating, stirring occasionally to separate. Remove to a paper towel or cloth to drain.

Place in a warmed serving bowl and toss with Tomato Pancetta Butter. Top with the reserved pancetta and garnish with additional pecorino-Romano cheese and thyme sprigs.

You can prepare the ravioli in a ravioli form using the manufacturer's instructions if preferred.

Serves 6

Tomato Pancetta Butter

3 ounces thinly sliced pancetta or
   bacon, coarsely chopped
1/4 cup (1/2 stick) unsalted butter
4 oil-pack sun-dried tomatoes,
   drained and chopped,
   about 2 tablespoons
1/2 teaspoon minced fresh thyme
freshly ground pepper to taste

Sauté the pancetta in a medium sauté pan over medium-high heat for 3 to 5 minutes or until crisp and brown. Remove to a paper towel with a slotted spoon to cool. Reserve 2 tablespoons of the pancetta. Combine the remaining pancetta with the butter, sun-dried tomatoes, thyme and pepper in a saucepan. Cook until the butter melts, stirring constantly. Keep warm.

Makes about 1 cup

Pesto Pizza

chopped fresh basil
3 garlic cloves
1/3 cup (about) grated
   Parmesan cheese
1/2 cup (about) extra-virgin olive oil
salt to taste
1 prepared pizza crust
shredded mozzarella cheese
baby spinach leaves
1 (15-ounce) can diced
   tomatoes, drained
chopped broccoli florets, zucchini,
   parsley or other vegetables of
   choice (optional)
1 tablespoon bread crumbs
1 to 2 teaspoons Italian seasoning,
   or a mixture of oregano
   and rosemary

Combine the basil, garlic, Parmesan cheese, olive oil and salt in a food processor or blender. Process until smooth. Spread over the pizza crust and top with mozzarella cheese, spinach, tomatoes and other vegetables preferred. Sprinkle with the bread crumbs and Italian seasoning. Bake at 375 degrees until the cheese melts. Broil 4 inches from the heat source for 2 to 3 minutes or until the bread crumbs are golden brown and crisp.

Serves 2

AuraPro Frittata with Onions and Red Bell Peppers

THANKS TO WHOLE FOODS MARKET

2   tablespoons canola oil
1   pound Italian-sausage flavor
    AuraPro
1   cup chopped yellow onion
1   cup chopped red bell pepper
1   teaspoon chopped garlic
8   eggs
sea salt and freshly ground pepper
    to taste
3   fresh herb sprigs, such as basil,
    tarragon or chervil, chopped
1   cup (4 ounces) shredded
    Chihuahua cheese

Heat the canola oil in a nonstick sauté pan over medium heat. Crumble the AuraPro into the sauté pan and sauté for 2 to 3 minutes. Add the onion, bell pepper and garlic and sauté for 3 minutes. Reduce the heat to low.

Whisk the eggs with the sea salt and pepper in a mixing bowl. Stir into the sauté pan. Cook until the bottom and side of the eggs are set and light brown. Sprinkle with the herbs and Chihuahua cheese, pressing them lightly into the frittata with a spatula.

Slide the frittata onto a plate and invert back into the sauté pan. Cook for 2 to 3 minutes longer or until the bottom is firm and light brown, shaking the pan constantly to prevent sticking.

AuraPro is a wheat-and soy bean-based protein alternative that comes in different flavors. St. Louis has pioneered in the use of these tasteful alternatives to meat with an appeal beyond vegetarians to health-conscious diners.

Serves 4 to 6

Risotto with Fresh Asparagus

THANKS TO DOMINIC'S

5 cups chicken stock
1 small onion, finely chopped
3 tablespoons olive oil
1/2 tomato, peeled and chopped
8 ounces fresh asparagus, chopped
2 ounces prosciutto or cooked ham, chopped into 1/2-inch pieces
2 cups arborio rice
5 tablespoons butter
3/4 cup (3 ounces) grated Parmesan cheese
salt and pepper to taste

Bring the chicken stock to a simmer in a saucepan and maintain at a simmer. Sauté the onion in the hot olive oil in a large skillet until tender. Add the tomato, asparagus and prosciutto and sauté for 5 minutes. Add the rice, stirring to coat evenly. Cook for 1 to 2 minutes.

Add the hot chicken stock one ladleful at a time, cooking until the liquid is absorbed after each addition and stirring constantly with a wooden spoon; the process will require about 10 minutes. Remove from the heat and add the butter and cheese, stirring gently until melted. Season with salt and pepper and serve immediately.

Serves 6

It takes no fewer than fifteen people every day to put *Show Me St. Louis* on the air.

Dining In

Dining In

Toasted Barley Risotto with Mustard Greens and Parsnips

THANKS TO THE KELLY TWINS

1/4 cup olive oil
1 1/2 cups pearled barley or farro
1/2 cup sliced shallots
2 cups peeled and chopped
(1/2-inch pieces) parsnips
2 teaspoons dried thyme
sea salt and freshly ground pepper
to taste
5 cups (or more) vegetable stock
or chicken stock
1 fresh bay leaf
3 cups blanched and shredded
mustard greens, kale or
Swiss chard
3/4 cup (3 ounces) grated
Parmesan cheese (optional)

Heat the olive oil in a heavy saucepan and add the barley. Sauté over medium-low heat until the barley is toasted to a golden brown. Add the shallots, parsnips, thyme, sea salt and pepper. Sauté until the shallots and parsnips are golden brown. Stir in the vegetable stock and bay leaf.

Bring to a boil and reduce the heat to a simmer. Cook, covered, for 30 minutes or until the barley is tender. Stir in the mustard greens and cook until heated through. Adjust the seasoning. Fold in the Parmesan cheese and add additional vegetable stock if desired for a creamier consistency. Remove the bay leaf before serving.

Farro is a highly nutritious full-flavored grain with a long history in the Middle East, North Africa and Italy.

Serves 6

Corn Bread Stuffing

2 cups chopped celery
1 cup chopped onion
1/2 cup (1 stick) butter, melted
4 cups crumbled corn bread
1/2 cup chopped green bell pepper
1/2 cup slivered almonds
1 cup sliced water chestnuts
1 tablespoon poultry seasoning
1 teaspoon sugar
1 teaspoon salt
1 teaspoon pepper

Sauté the celery and onion in the butter in a large skillet over medium heat for 3 minutes. Add the corn bread, bell pepper, almonds, water chestnuts, poultry seasoning, sugar, salt and pepper and mix well.

Use as stuffing for a 10-pound turkey.

Serves 10 to 12

Show Me St. Louis has traveled to places like Syracuse, NY, Orlando, FL, Minneapolis, MN, and Kansas City, MO, for stories for the program.

Desserts

Busch Stadium

Now I have a family, which is good for me because I have someone to love. I would tell other kids who are waiting to keep praying to have a family, so someone can love you. Don't give up, because someone is waiting for you.

Darrell, age 12, adopted

Kids who have been in foster care need positive ways to express their feelings. Darrell was always artistic, but never had any formal training. For his Little Wish, Darrell requested art lessons at a prestigious local art school. After a few weeks of classes, Darrell was able to realize his talent, giving him the colorful, creative outlet he needed.

Caramel Apple Crisp

THANKS TO NICHE

2 cups sugar
1/4 cup corn syrup
1/4 cup water
1/2 cup heavy cream
6 Granny Smith apples,
   peeled and sliced
2 tablespoons cornstarch
2 tablespoons cold water
Almond Oat Topping (below)

Whisk the sugar, corn syrup and 1/4 cup water together in a saucepan. Cook over medium heat until it forms an amber-colored syrup; do not stir. Remove from the heat and whisk in the cream carefully. Return to the heat and add the apples. Cook until the apples are slightly tender.

Blend the cornstarch with 2 tablespoons cold water in a cup. Add to the apple mixture and cook until thickened, stirring constantly. Spoon into a square baking dish and top with Almond Oat Topping. Bake at 400 degrees for 25 to 30 minutes or until golden brown and bubbly. Serve warm with a scoop of ice cream.

Serves 6

Almond Oat Topping

THANKS TO NICHE

1 1/3 cups rolled oats
2/3 cup all-purpose flour
1/3 cup granulated sugar
1/3 cup packed brown sugar
2/3 cup toasted almonds
1/8 teaspoon salt
3/4 cup (1 1/2 sticks) butter, melted

Mix the oats, flour, granulated sugar, brown sugar, almonds and salt in a bowl. Add the butter and mix with a fork. Store in the refrigerator until needed.

Makes 3 cups

Apple Crumble Dessert

1   (2-layer) package yellow
     cake mix
1 1/4 cups rolled oats
1/2   cup (1 stick) butter
     or margarine
1   egg
4   Granny Smith apples, peeled
     and sliced
3/4   cup packed brown sugar
1/2   cup chopped pecans

Mix the cake mix and oats in a bowl. Add the butter and cut into the mixture with a pastry blender or fork until the mixture resembles coarse crumbs. Reserve 1 cup of the mixture for the topping.

Add the egg to the remaining crumb mixture; mix well. Press over the bottom of a 9×13-inch baking pan sprayed with nonstick cooking spray.

Combine the apples, brown sugar and pecans in a bowl and mix well. Spoon into the prepared pan and sprinkle the reserved crumb mixture over the top. Bake at 375 degrees for 30 to 35 minutes or until golden brown. Serve with ice cream if desired.

Serves 12

Dining In

Bread Pudding

THANKS TO SOULARD'S RESTAURANT

3   eggs
1   cup sugar
2   to 2¹/₂ cups milk
1¹/₂ teaspoons ground cinnamon
¹/₂   teaspoon nutmeg
2   teaspoons vanilla extract
4   apples, peeled and sliced
4   peaches, peeled and sliced
6¹/₂ cups cubed day-old French or
     Italian bread
6   tablespoons butter,
     cut into small pieces
Whiskey Sauce (below)

Beat the eggs with the sugar, milk, cinnamon, nutmeg and vanilla in a large mixing bowl until smooth. Add the apples and peaches and mix gently. Add the bread and toss to coat. Spoon into a 9×13-inch baking dish sprayed with nonstick cooking spray. Top with the butter and bake at 350 degrees for 1 hour. Serve warm topped with Whiskey Sauce.

Serves 12

Whiskey Sauce

THANKS TO SOULARD'S RESTAURANT

1   cup whiskey
1   pound (4 sticks) butter
2   cups sugar

Combine the whiskey, butter and sugar in a saucepan. Cook over medium heat until the sugar melts and the mixture is heated through, whisking constantly. Serve warm.

Makes 4 cups

Chocolate Marble Cheesecake

1 1/2 cups graham cracker crumbs
6   tablespoons butter, melted
1/4 cup sugar
3   ounces unsweetened
     chocolate
1   teaspoon shortening
32   ounces cream cheese,
     softened
2   teaspoons vanilla extract
1 1/2 cups sugar
6   eggs, lightly beaten
2   cups light cream, or 1 cup
     heavy cream and 1 cup milk

Mix the graham cracker crumbs with the butter and 1/4 cup sugar in a bowl. Press over the bottom and halfway up the side of a greased springform pan.

Melt the chocolate with the shortening in a double boiler over simmering water, stirring to blend well. Beat the cream cheese with the vanilla in a large mixing bowl until light and fluffy. Beat in 1 1/2 cups sugar gradually. Add the eggs and beat just until blended. Stir in the cream. Remove 3 cups of the cream cheese mixture to a second bowl and reserve. Spoon the remaining mixture into the prepared crust.

Add the chocolate to the reserved cream cheese mixture. Spoon onto the top of the cheesecake filling in three mounds. Swirl a knife or spatula through the mixture in a zigzag pattern. Bake at 450 degrees until the center is nearly set. Cool to room temperature and chill in the refrigerator. Place on a serving plate and remove the side of the pan to serve.

Serves 12

Cake Crème Brûlée

THANKS TO NICHE

3 egg yolks
1/4 cup sugar
1/2 vanilla bean
1 cup cream
1/2 loaf pound cake, cut into cubes and toasted

Whisk the egg yolks, sugar and vanilla in a bowl until combined. Heat the cream to a simmer in a small saucepan. Stir the hot cream into the egg mixture gradually. Remove the vanilla bean. Place seven cake cubes in each of six baking ramekins and pour the cream mixture over the cubes. Place in a baking pan and add 1/2 inch water to the pan. Cover the ramekins with foil and bake at 300 degrees for 45 to 60 minutes or until set. Serve with sliced fruit or jam.

Serves 6

Pumpkin Crème Brûlée

THANKS TO J. BUCK'S

1/4 cup sugar
1 cup milk
1 cup 40% heavy cream
5 egg yolks
1/2 cup pumpkin purée
1/4 teaspoon nutmeg
1/4 teaspoon ground cinnamon
1/8 teaspoon salt
2 egg whites, stiffly beaten
cinnamon-sugar for the topping

Mix the sugar with the milk and cream in a saucepan. Bring just to a boil, stirring to avoid scorching. Remove from the heat and cool. Chill in the refrigerator.

Beat the egg yolks in a bowl until doubled in volume. Fold in the pumpkin purée, nutmeg, cinnamon and salt. Fold in the egg whites and chilled cream mixture.

Spoon into ramekins or soufflé cups. Place in a baking pan and add 1/2 inch water to the pan. Bake at 275 degrees for 30 to 60 minutes or until set. Remove to a wire rack and cool to room temperature. Chill in the refrigerator. Sprinkle a mixture of cinnamon-sugar on the tops and caramelize under a broiler or with a kitchen torch.

Serves 6

Peach Cobbler

THANKS TO THE KITCHEN CONSERVATORY

12 cups sliced peeled peaches
4 teaspoons cornstarch
2/3 cup sugar
1/4 teaspoon nutmeg
1/2 teaspoon ground ginger
1/2 teaspoon almond extract
1 cup all-purpose flour
1/2 teaspoon baking powder
1/8 teaspoon salt
1 cup (2 sticks) butter, softened
1 cup sugar
1 egg
1/2 teaspoon vanilla extract

Combine the peaches with the cornstarch, 2/3 cup sugar, the nutmeg, ginger and almond extract in a bowl and mix well. Spoon into one large or two 8×8-inch baking pans.

Mix the flour, baking powder and salt together. Cream the butter and 1 cup sugar in a mixing bowl until light and fluffy. Beat in the egg and vanilla. Fold in the flour mixture just until mixed. Drop by heaping tablespoonfuls onto the peach mixture. Bake at 375 degrees for 45 minutes or until golden brown.

Serves 16

Dining In

Former reporter Wendy Bell is now the main anchor at WTAE-TV in Pittsburgh, Pennsylvania.

Tiramisu

THANKS TO DOMINIC'S

6 egg yolks
1 cup sugar
12 ounces mascarpone cheese
1 tablespoon sambuco
6 egg whites
1 cup brewed espresso
1/4 cup sweet marsala
36 ladyfingers
3 ounces semisweet
    chocolate, grated
baking cocoa for garnish

Beat the egg yolks with the sugar, mascarpone cheese and liqueur in a mixing bowl until creamy. Beat the egg whites in a bowl until soft peaks form. Fold into the cheese mixture.

Mix the espresso and wine in a bowl and dip the ladyfingers into the mixture one at a time. Arrange half the ladyfingers in a single layer in a rectangular glass bowl. Spread half the cheese mixture over the ladyfingers. Layer the remaining ladyfingers over the cheese mixture, arranging them in the opposite direction as the first layer. Top with the remaining cheese mixture and sprinkle with the grated chocolate. Garnish with the baking cocoa. Chill for 4 hours before serving.

You can substitute seasonal berries for the baking cocoa as a topping if you prefer.

If you are concerned about using raw eggs, use eggs pasteurized in their shells, which are sold at some specialty food stores, or use an equivalent amount of pasteurized egg substitute.

Serves 8

Death by Chocolate

THANKS TO THE BLUE OWL RESTAURANT & BAKERY

1 (21-ounce) package fudge brownie mix
1/3 to 1/2 cup Kahlúa or other coffee liqueur
3 (3-ounce) packages chocolate mousse mix
6 (1-ounce) chocolate-covered toffee bars
24 ounces whipped topping

Prepare and bake the brownies using the package directions for a 9×13-inch baking dish. Let cool to room temperature. Pierce holes in the brownies with a fork and pour the liqueur over the top. Prepare the chocolate mousse using the package directions. Break the candy bars into small pieces and reserve 1/4 cup of the pieces for the top. Mix the remaining candy pieces with the whipped topping in a bowl.

Alternate layers of the whipped topping mixture and the chocolate mousse over the brownies, ending with the whipped topping. Sprinkle the reserved candy on the top. Store in the refrigerator.

This recipe was tested with Jell-O chocolate mousse and Heath candy bars.

Serves 20

Dessert Pizza

THANKS TO FORTEL'S PIZZA DEN

1/2 cup all-purpose flour
1/2 cup packed brown sugar
1/4 cup (1/2 stick) butter, softened
1 tablespoon cinnamon
1 pizza crust, partially baked
1 (21-ounce) can pie filling of choice
3/4 cup confectioners' sugar
1 tablespoon (or more) milk
1/16 teaspoon salt
1/16 teaspoon vanilla extract

Mix the flour, brown sugar, butter and cinnamon with a pastry blender in a medium bowl until pea-size crumbs form. Place the pizza crust on a work surface. Spread the pie filling to the edge of the crust. Sprinkle the crumb mixture over the top.

Place the pizza directly on the oven rack or on a pizza stone. Bake at 450 degrees for 5 to 10 minutes or until the topping is brown. Blend the confectioners' sugar, milk, salt and vanilla in a small bowl, adding additional milk if needed for the desired consistency. Drizzle over the warm pizza and cut into wedges to serve immediately.

Serves 8

Desserts

Monkey Bread Sweet Rolls

1   (16-ounce) package frozen
    yeast rolls
1/2 cup granulated sugar
1/2 teaspoon ground cinnamon
1/2 cup chopped walnuts
1/2 cup packed light brown sugar
10   tablespoons butter, cut into
     1/2-tablespoon pieces

Arrange the frozen roll dough flat side down in a bundt pan or tube pan sprayed with nonstick cooking spray. Mix the granulated sugar and cinnamon in a small bowl and sprinkle over the rolls. Sprinkle with the walnuts and brown sugar. Dot with the butter. Cover with plastic wrap and place in a cold oven or other draft-free place. Let rise for 8 hours or longer.

Bake the rolls, uncovered, at 350 degrees for 30 minutes or until golden brown and bubbly. Let stand in the pan for 10 minutes. Place a plate over the top of the pan and invert the sweet rolls onto the plate; shake the pan if necessary to release the rolls. Serve warm or at room temperature by pulling the rolls apart. Store, covered with plastic wrap and foil, at room temperature for up to 3 days.

Serves 12

The most requested recipe on our program by our viewers has been Debbye Turner's Apple Cake recipe.

Apple Cake

2³/4 cups all-purpose flour
1   teaspoon baking soda
1   teaspoon ground cinnamon
1   teaspoon nutmeg
1   teaspoon salt
3   cups chopped peeled
     Jonathan apples
1   cup nuts
1   cup flaked coconut
1/4 cup all-purpose flour
3   eggs
1¹/2 cups vegetable oil
2   cups sugar
2   teaspoons vanilla extract
Brown Sugar Glaze (below)

Sift 2³/4 cups flour with the baking soda, cinnamon, nutmeg and salt. Toss the apples, nuts and coconut with 1/4 cup flour in a bowl, coating evenly.

Beat the eggs in a mixing bowl until light. Add the oil, sugar and vanilla and beat until smooth. Stir in the flour mixture. Fold in the apple mixture. Spoon into a greased and floured bundt pan. Bake at 350 degrees for 60 to 70 minutes or until a cake tester comes out clean.

Let the cake stand in the pan for 5 minutes. Pour hot Brown Sugar Glaze over the cake in the pan. Let stand for several minutes. Remove the cake to a plate.

You can reserve 1/3 to 1/2 cup of the glaze to pour over the cake after removing it from the pan if desired.

Serves 12

Brown Sugar Glaze

1   cup packed brown sugar
1/3 cup butter or margarine
1/4 cup milk
1   teaspoon vanilla extract

Mix the brown sugar, butter, milk and vanilla in a small saucepan. Boil for 2 minutes, stirring frequently.

Makes 1 1/2 cups

Must-Bake Carrot Cake

2 1/2 cups all-purpose flour
1 1/2 teaspoons baking powder
1 1/2 teaspoons baking soda
2 teaspoons ground cinnamon
1/2 teaspoon salt
1 1/2 cups packed brown sugar
1 cup drained crushed pineapple
3/4 cup fat-free egg substitute, or
3 eggs
3/4 cup buttermilk
1/2 cup unsweetened applesauce
1/3 cup vegetable oil
2 teaspoons vanilla extract
3 cups grated carrots
1/2 cup chopped walnuts
Cheater's Frosting (below)

Mix the flour, baking powder, baking soda, cinnamon and salt together. Combine the brown sugar, pineapple, egg substitute, buttermilk, applesauce, oil and vanilla in a bowl and whisk to mix well. Stir in the carrots. Add the flour mixture and mix well. Stir in the walnuts.

Spoon into a 9×13-inch cake pan sprayed with nonstick cooking spray. Bake at 350 degrees for 35 to 40 minutes or until a cake tester inserted in the center comes out clean. Cool in the pan on a wire rack. Spread Cheater's Frosting over the top. Store, covered with plastic wrap, in the refrigerator.

Serves 24

Cheater's Frosting

1 (16-ounce) container low-fat vanilla frosting
1 teaspoon grated orange zest
1 tablespoon thawed frozen orange juice concentrate

Combine the prepared frosting, orange zest and orange juice concentrate in a bowl and mix well. Store, covered, in the refrigerator until needed.

This recipe was tested with Betty Crocker frosting.

Frosts 1 cake

Almond Joy Cake

1 (2-layer) package chocolate
   cake mix with pudding
1 cup sugar
14 ounces flaked coconut
24 large marshmallows
1 cup evaporated milk
1/2 cup (1 stick) butter or margarine
1/2 cup evaporated milk
1 1/2 cups (9 ounces) chocolate chips
sliced almonds

Prepare and bake the cake mix using the package directions for a 9×13-inch cake pan. Combine the sugar, coconut, marshmallows and 1 cup evaporated milk in a saucepan. Cook over medium heat until the marshmallows melt, stirring constantly. Pour the mixture over the hot cake. Cool the cake at room temperature for 1 hour or chill in the refrigerator for 30 minutes.

Combine the butter with 1/2 cup evaporated milk in a saucepan. Bring to a boil and stir in the chocolate chips until melted. Spread over the marshmallow layer and sprinkle with almonds. Chill in the refrigerator for 8 hours or longer.

Serves 16

Show Me St. Louis has put on more than 2,600 shows in its eleven-year history.

Chocolate Chip Cake

4   ounces German's sweet
    chocolate
1   (2-layer) package yellow
    cake mix
1   (3-ounce) package vanilla
    instant pudding mix
1   cup milk
1   cup vegetable oil
4   eggs
1   cup (6 ounces) semisweet
    chocolate chips

Break the German's chocolate into four pieces. Grate the chocolate finely one piece at a time in a food processor or with a hand grater.

Combine the cake mix, pudding mix, milk, oil and eggs in a large mixing bowl and beat at low speed for 1 minute. Fold in the grated chocolate and scrape down the side of the bowl with a rubber spatula. Increase the speed to medium and beat for 2 minutes longer, scraping down the side if necessary. Fold in the chocolate chips.

Spoon the batter into a 10-inch tube pan sprayed lightly with nonstick spray and coated with flour; smooth the batter with a rubber spatula. Bake at 325 degrees on the center oven rack for 58 to 60 minutes or until the top is golden brown and springs back when lightly pressed with your finger. Cool in the pan on a wire rack for 20 minutes.

Loosen the cake from the side of the pan with a long sharp knife and invert it onto the rack. Cool for 30 minutes. Store, wrapped in foil or plastic wrap, at room temperature for up to 1 week or in the freezer for up to 6 months.

You can bake the batter in three 8-inch loaf pans if preferred. Reduce the cooking time to 50 to 52 minutes and cool in the pans for 5 minutes.

Serves 16

Simply Elegant
Chocolate Cake

THANKS TO THE MISSOURI EGG COUNCIL

2 cups (12 ounces) semisweet chocolate chips
1 cup (2 sticks) unsalted butter, cut into pieces
1/4 cup water
1/2 teaspoon instant coffee granules
1/2 cup baking cocoa
1/3 cup sugar
8 eggs
confectioners' sugar for dusting
sweetened whipped cream

Grease the bottom of a 9-inch springform pan. Line the bottom with baking parchment and grease the parchment. Combine the chocolate chips, butter, water and instant coffee granules in a large heavy saucepan. Cook over low heat until the butter and chocolate chips melt, stirring to blend well. Stir in the cocoa and sugar; remove from the heat.

Beat the eggs in a large mixing bowl for 5 minutes or until doubled in volume. Fold into the batter one-third at a time, mixing until smooth after each addition. Spoon into the prepared springform pan.

Bake at 325 degrees for 30 to 35 minutes or until the edges are firm and shiny; the center will not be completely firm. Cool in the pan on a wire rack; the center will sink slightly. Cover and store in the refrigerator for 4 hours or for up to 4 days.

Loosen the side of the springform pan with a knife about 30 minutes before serving. Invert the cake onto baking parchment and remove the parchment liner. Invert onto a cake plate. Dust with confectioners' sugar and top each serving with a dollop of sweetened whipped cream.

Serves 12

Dining In

Milky Way Cake

4   (2-ounce) Milky Way
    candy bars
1/2 cup (1 stick) butter
    or margarine
1 1/2 cups all-purpose flour
1/2 teaspoon baking soda
1   teaspoon salt
2   cups sugar
3/4 cup vegetable oil
4   eggs
1   cup buttermilk
2   teaspoons vanilla extract
1   cup pecans or walnuts
Milky Way Frosting (below)

Combine the candy bars and butter in a double boiler and heat over simmering water until melted; cool to room temperature. Sift the flour, baking soda and salt together.

Combine the sugar, oil, eggs and buttermilk in a bowl and mix well. Add the flour mixture and beat for 2 minutes or until smooth. Beat in the vanilla and cooled candy mixture. Stir in the pecans.

Spoon into a tube pan or 9×13-inch cake pan sprayed with nonstick cooking spray. Bake at 325 degrees for 1 1/4 hours. Cool the cake on a wire rack. Spread with Milky Way Frosting.

You can microwave the candy in a deep microwave-safe bowl on Medium for 4 minutes. Add the melted butter and microwave on High for 1 minute. Beat with an electric mixer until smooth.

Serves 16

Milky Way Frosting

2   (2-ounce) Milky Way
    candy bars
1/2 cup (1 stick) butter
    or margarine
2   teaspoons milk
1/2 (16-ounce) package
    confectioners' sugar

Combine the candy bars and butter in a double boiler and heat over simmering water until melted. Cool to room temperature and add the milk and confectioners' sugar; beat until smooth. Adjust the confectioners' sugar or milk if needed for the desired consistency.

You can microwave the candy in a deep microwave-safe bowl on Medium for 2 minutes. Add the melted butter and microwave on High for 1 minute. Beat with an electric mixer until smooth.

Serves 16

Upside-Down German Chocolate Cake

1 1/2 cups pecans pieces
3/4 cup flaked coconut
1 (2-layer) package German chocolate cake mix
3 eggs
1 1/4 cups water
1/2 cup vegetable oil
8 ounces cream cheese, softened
1 (16-ounce) package confectioners' sugar
1 cup (2 sticks) margarine, melted and cooled

Sprinkle the pecans and coconut in a greased and floured 9×13-inch baking pan. Combine the cake mix with the eggs, water and vegetable oil, using the package directions. Spread in the prepared baking pan.

Combine the cream cheese, sugar and margarine in a mixing bowl and beat until smooth; the mixture will be thick. Spoon over the cake batter and carefully spread to an even layer.

Bake at 350 degrees for 50 to 55 minutes or until the cakes pulls away from the sides of the pan. Cool on a wire rack. Invert onto a foil-covered tray or serving platter.

Serves 16

Show Me St. Louis has done more than fifty stories at the Science Center.

Turtle Cake

1 (2-layer) package German
 chocolate cake mix
40 caramels
1/3 cup evaporated skim milk
1 cup pecans
1 cup (6 ounces) chocolate chips

Prepare the cake mix using the package directions. Spread half the batter in a greased 9×13-inch baking pan. Bake at 350 degrees for 15 minutes.

Combine the caramels with the evaporated milk in a saucepan or microwave-safe bowl. Heat until melted or microwave on High for 2 to 4 minutes, stirring to blend evenly. Pour the mixture over the cake and sprinkle with the pecans and chocolate chips.

Spread the remaining cake batter evenly over the top. Bake for 15 to 25 minutes or until the top appears firm. Serve with ice cream.

Serves 16

Lemon Blueberry Cake

1 (2-layer) package yellow
 cake mix
1 tablespoon grated lemon zest
2 cups fresh or frozen blueberries
1 1/2 cups water
1 (6-ounce) package
 lemon gelatin
confectioners' sugar for dusting
8 ounces whipped topping

Prepare the cake mix using the package directions and adding the lemon zest. Spoon the batter into a 9×13-inch cake pan lightly sprayed with nonstick cooking spray. Sprinkle with the blueberries.

Place the water in a microwave-safe bowl and microwave on High until boiling. Whisk in the gelatin until dissolved completely. Pour evenly over the blueberries. Bake at 375 degrees for 30 to 35 minutes or until a wooden pick inserted into the center comes out clean. Cool slightly and dust with confectioners' sugar. Top with the whipped topping to serve.

Serves 1

Pumpkin Gooey Butter Cake

THANKS TO THE MISSOURI EGG COUNCIL

1	(2-layer) package yellow cake mix
1	egg
1/2	cup (1 stick) butter, melted
8	ounces cream cheese, softened
1	(15-ounce) can pumpkin
3	eggs
1/2	cup (1 stick) butter, melted
1	teaspoon vanilla extract
1	(16-ounce) package confectioners' sugar
1	teaspoon ground cinnamon
1	teaspoon nutmeg

Combine the cake mix, 1 egg and 1/2 cup melted butter in a bowl and beat until mixed. Press into a lightly greased 9×13-inch baking pan.

Beat the cream cheese with the pumpkin in a mixing bowl until smooth. Add 3 eggs, 1/2 cup melted butter and the vanilla and beat until well mixed. Add the confectioners' sugar, cinnamon and nutmeg and mix well.

Spread the pumpkin mixture over the prepared layer. Bake at 350 degrees for 40 to 50 minutes or just until the edges are firm; do not overbake, as the center should be a little gooey.

Serves 6 to 8

Dining In

Candy Cane Cookies

1/2 cup crushed peppermint
candy canes or hard
peppermint candies
1/2 cup granulated sugar
1/2 cup (1 stick) butter or
margarine, softened
1/2 cup shortening or butter-
flavor shortening
1 cup confectioners' sugar
1 egg
1 teaspoon vanilla extract
1/2 teaspoon peppermint extract
2 1/2 cups all-purpose flour
1/2 teaspoon red food coloring

Mix the peppermint candy and granulated sugar in a bowl. Combine the butter, shortening, confectioners' sugar, egg, vanilla and peppermint extract in a large bowl. Beat at medium-high speed for 2 to 3 minutes or until light and fluffy. Add the flour gradually, beating constantly at medium-low speed to mix well. Remove half the dough to a sheet of waxed paper. Add the red food coloring to the dough remaining in the bowl and beat until evenly distributed.

Roll 1 teaspoonful of each dough into 4-inch ropes. Twist the ropes together and shape into canes. Repeat with the remaining dough, arranging the canes 1 inch apart on two ungreased baking sheets.

Place in a 375-degree oven on oven racks adjusted to divide the oven into even thirds. Bake for 9 minutes or until very light golden brown and firm to the touch, reversing the direction of the baking sheets once during the baking time. Sprinkle immediately with the peppermint candy mixture. Remove to wire racks with a wide spatula to cool. Store in an airtight container, separating the layers with waxed paper.

You can wrap the dough in foil and store it in the refrigerator for up to one week or in the freezer for up to three months. Thaw frozen dough in the refrigerator and bring the dough to room temperature before using.

Makes 2 dozen

Chocolate-Covered Cherry Cookies

1½ cups all-purpose flour
½ cup baking cocoa
¼ teaspoon baking soda
¼ teaspoon salt
½ cup (1 stick) butter or margarine, softened
1 cup sugar
1 egg
1½ teaspoons vanilla extract
1 (10-ounce) jar maraschino cherries, 48 cherries
16 ounces chocolate chips
½ cup sweetened condensed milk

Mix the flour, cocoa, baking soda and salt together. Cream the butter and sugar at low speed in a mixing bowl until fluffy. Beat in the egg and vanilla. Add the flour mixture gradually, mixing well after each addition.

Shape the dough into 1½-inch balls. Arrange on a greased cookie sheet. Press the center of each cookie to make an indentation. Drain the cherries, reserving the juice. Place a cherry in the center of each cookie.

Cook the chocolate chips and sweetened condensed milk in a saucepan until the chocolate melts, stirring to blend well. Stir in 4 to 6 teaspoons of the reserved cherry juice, adding more if needed for the desired consistency. Spoon 1 teaspoon of the mixture over each cookie.

Bake at 350 degrees for 10 minutes. Cool on the cookie sheet for several minutes, then remove to a wire rack to cool completely.

Makes 4 dozen

We've married six couples on our show.

Chocolate Walnut Drops

2 eggs
2 teaspoons vanilla extract
1 cup (2 sticks) butter, softened
2 cups packed brown sugar
1/2 cup baking cocoa
2 cups all-purpose flour
2 teaspoons baking soda
4 cups walnuts

Beat the eggs with the vanilla in a bowl. Cream the butter and brown sugar in a mixing bowl until light and fluffy. Add the baking cocoa and mix well. Add the egg mixture and mix well. Add the flour and baking soda and mix until smooth. Mix in the walnuts. Drop by spoonfuls about 2 inches apart onto a nonstick cookie sheet.

Bake at 350 degrees for 12 to 15 minutes or just until golden brown. Cool on the cookie sheet for several minutes, then remove to a wire rack to cool completely.

You may add 1/2 cup granulated sugar with the brown sugar if a slightly sweeter cookie is preferred.

Makes 3 dozen

Miniature Morsel Meringue Cookies

THANKS TO THE MISSOURI EGG COUNCIL

4 egg whites
1/2 teaspoon cream of tartar
1 cup ultra-fine sugar
2 cups (12 ounces) miniature semisweet chocolate chips

Beat the egg whites with the cream of tartar in a large mixing bowl until soft peaks form. Add the sugar gradually, beating constantly until stiff peaks form. Fold in the chocolate chips one-third at a time.

Drop the mixture by level teaspoonfuls onto greased cookie sheets. Bake at 300 degrees for 20 to 25 minutes or until the cookies are dry and crisp. Cool on the cookie sheets for 2 minutes, then remove to wire racks to cool completely. Store in an airtight container.

Makes 4 dozen

The Very Best Cookies

THANKS TO THE VERY BEST COOKIES

1 cup (2 sticks) margarine, softened
1 1/2 cups sugar
1 egg
1 teaspoon vanilla extract
2 1/2 cups all-purpose flour
1 teaspoon baking soda
1 teaspoon cream of tartar
colored sugar, cinnamon–sugar or additional plain sugar for coating

Combine the margarine, 1 1/2 cups sugar, the egg and vanilla in a mixing bowl and beat at medium speed for 4 minutes or until light. Add the flour, baking soda and cream of tartar, beating at low speed just until moistened. Place the dough in a covered container and chill in the refrigerator for 30 minutes or longer.

Roll some of the dough into twelve 1-inch balls and place in a 1-gallon sealable plastic bag with colored sugar; shake lightly to coat evenly. Repeat with the remaining dough.

Arrange the dough balls on a cookie sheet lined with baking parchment. Bake at 350 degrees for 10 minutes or just until light golden brown. Cool on the cookie sheet for several minutes, then remove to a wire rack to cool completely.

You can vary the color of the coating sugar to match the season. Use six parts sugar to one part ground cinnamon to produce a cookie called a snickerdoodle.

Makes 7 dozen

Dining In

Chocolate-Crusted Coconut Bars

THANKS TO THE MISSOURI EGG COUNCIL

1 1/2 cups all-purpose flour
1/4 cup sugar
2 tablespoons baking cocoa
1/2 cup (1 stick) unsalted butter, cubed and softened
4 cups unsweetened flaked coconut
8 egg whites
2 cups confectioners' sugar
1/2 cup sweetened cream of coconut
2 ounces bittersweet chocolate, melted

Combine the flour, sugar and cocoa in a food processor. Add the butter one cube at a time, pulsing until the mixture forms a dough. Roll the dough to a 9×13-inch rectangle between two sheets of waxed paper. Peel off one sheet of the waxed paper and fit the dough into a 9×13-inch baking pan sprayed with nonstick cooking spray. Peel off the remaining waxed paper. Prick the dough with a fork and place in the refrigerator. Mix the coconut, egg whites, confectioners' sugar and cream of coconut in a bowl. Press lightly over the crust.

Bake at 375 degrees on the center oven rack for 15 minutes or just until set. Cool on a wire rack and cut into 3×3-inch bars. Drizzle with the melted chocolate.

Makes 1 dozen

Fat-Free Chocolate Fudge Brownies

3/4 cup unsweetened apple butter
1 cup granulated sugar
1 cup packed brown sugar
1 cup egg substitute
2 teaspoons vanilla extract
1 cup all-purpose flour
1/2 teaspoon baking powder
3/4 cup baking cocoa
confectioners' sugar for dusting

Combine the apple butter, granulated sugar, brown sugar, egg substitute and vanilla in a large bowl and mix until smooth. Add the flour, baking powder and baking cocoa and mix well. Spoon into a 9×13-inch baking dish sprayed with nonstick cooking spray. Bake at 350 degrees for 30 to 35 minutes or until the brownies test done. Cool to room temperature on a wire rack and dust with confectioners' sugar if desired. Cut into squares.

Makes 2 dozen

Chocolate Pecan Squares

1/2 cup (1 stick) margarine, softened
1/4 cup sugar
1 1/4 cups all-purpose flour
1/2 cup sugar
1/4 cup (1/2 stick) margarine
2 tablespoons heavy cream
1 3/4 cups coarsely chopped pecans or walnuts
1 cup flaked coconut
4 ounces semisweet chocolate, coarsely chopped

Cream 1/2 cup margarine with 1/4 cup sugar in a mixing bowl until light. Beat in the flour. Press over the bottom of a 9×9-inch baking pan. Bake at 350 degrees for 18 minutes or until the edges are light brown.

Combine 1/2 cup sugar and 1/4 cup margarine with the cream in a saucepan. Cook until the margarine melts and the sugar dissolves, stirring constantly. Stir in the pecans.

Sprinkle the coconut and chocolate over the baked crust. Top with the pecan mixture. Bake for 20 minutes or until golden brown. Cool on a wire rack and cut into squares to serve.

Serves 16

Chocolate Raspberry Squares

3 cups crushed vanilla wafers or graham crackers
1/2 cup (1 stick) butter, melted
1/2 to 1 cup raspberry preserves
2 cups (12 ounces) white chocolate chips
8 ounces cream cheese, softened
2 cups (12 ounces) semisweet or milk chocolate chips

Mix the vanilla wafer crumbs with the melted butter in a bowl. Press over the bottom of a 9×13-inch baking pan. Bake at 350 degrees for 10 minutes. Cool on a wire rack. Spread the raspberry preserves evenly over the cooled crust.

Combine the white chocolate chops and cream cheese in a saucepan. Heat over low heat until melted, stirring to blend well. Spread evenly over the preserves. Melt the chocolate chips in a saucepan, stirring constantly. Spread over the cream cheese layer. Chill in the refrigerator until firm. Cut into squares.

You may want to let the squares stand at room temperature before serving.

Makes 2 dozen

Peanut Squares

THANKS TO ECKERT'S COUNTRY BAKERY

1 (2-layer) package yellow cake mix
3 cups confectioners' sugar
1/3 cup butter or margarine, softened
1/4 cup milk
1 1/2 teaspoons vanilla extract
16 ounces peanuts, crushed

Prepare and bake the cake mix in a 9×13-inch cake pan using the package directions. Freeze the cake in the pan for 8 hours or longer.

Combine the confectioners' sugar, butter, milk and vanilla in a bowl and beat until smooth; the mixture should be thin.

Cut the frozen cake into twelve 3×3-inch squares. Invert the pan to release the squares. Dip each square into the icing mixture, covering all four sides; remove any excess with a knife. Dip each square into the peanuts and press the peanuts lightly to all sides to adhere.

Makes 1 dozen

Sweet Cherry Bars

4 cups all-purpose flour
3/4 teaspoon baking soda
1/2 teaspoon salt
1 1/2 cups (3 sticks) unsalted butter, softened
1 1/2 cups granulated sugar
1 1/2 cups packed light brown sugar
3 eggs
1 teaspoon vanilla extract
2 cups stemmed halved pitted cherries
1/3 cup sliced almonds

Sift the flour with the baking soda and salt. Cream the butter with the granulated sugar and brown sugar in a mixing bowl until light and fluffy. Beat in the eggs one at a time. Stir in the vanilla. Add the flour mixture and mix well.

Spread half the batter in a buttered 9×13-inch baking pan. Sprinkle the cherries over the top. Dollop the remaining batter over the cherries and spread gently to cover the cherries evenly. Sprinkle with the almonds.

Bake at 350 degrees for 35 to 40 minues or until a tester inserted in the center comes out clean. Cool on a wire rack and cut into bars.

Makes 18

Black–Bottom Berry Tart

1 refrigerator pie pastry
6 ounces bittersweet chocolate,
   chopped, or semisweet
   chocolate chips
1/4 cup heavy cream
1 pint raspberries or strawberries
2 tablespoons raspberry jelly
   or red currant jelly
1 1/2 tablespoons cognac, raspberry
   liqueur or raspberry syrup

Place the pie pastry in a 9-inch tart pan with a removable bottom, folding the extra pastry under to reinforce the edge. Prick the bottom eight to ten times with a fork. Place in the freezer for 10 minutes. Bake at 425 degrees for 12 minutes or until light brown. Cool for 5 minutes or longer.

Place the chocolate in a double boiler and heat over simmering water until nearly melted. Remove from the heat and stir until smooth. Blend in the cream. Spread over the bottom of the tart shell. Arrange the berries stem side down in the chocolate, covering them completely. Chill for 10 minutes or until the chocolate is set.

Melt the jelly with the liqueur in a small saucepan and mix well. Brush over the berries. Serve immediately or store in the refrigerator for up to 6 hours.

You can melt the chocolate and the jelly mixture in the microwave if preferred.

Serves 4 to 6

White Chocolate Raspberry Tart

12 ounces white chocolate
1/2 cup cream
1/4 cup (1/2 stick) unsalted butter
2 cups fresh or individually
   frozen raspberries
1 baked (9-inch) tart shell, cooled

Microwave the white chocolate, cream and butter in a microwave-safe bowl on High for 1 minute. Stir and microwave longer if necessary to melt completely, stirring every 30 seconds. Arrange the raspberries in the tart shell. Pour the white chocolate mixture over the berries and chill until set.

You can melt an additional 1 ounce of white chocolate to brush over the tart shell if desired to prevent its becoming soggy. If using frozen berries, separate and drain them on paper towels.

Serves 6

Lemon Tart with Almond Crust

THANKS TO THE MISSOURI EGG COUNCIL

3 eggs
3 egg yolks
1 cup sugar
3/4 cup fresh lemon juice,
about 4 to 5 lemons
2 tablespoons grated lemon zest,
about 3 to 4 lemons
1/8 teaspoon salt
6 tablespoons unsalted
butter, cubed
Almond Crust (below)

Combine the eggs, egg yolks, sugar, lemon juice, lemon zest and salt in a large saucepan and whisk to mix well. Add the butter and cook for 8 to 10 minutes or to 160 degrees over medium-low heat, stirring constantly; the mixture should be thick enough to coat a metal spoon but still pourable.

Strain the mixture through a fine mesh sieve into the Almond Crust. Bake at 325 degrees for 10 minutes or just until the filling is set. Cool on a wire rack. Place on a serving plate and remove the side of the tart pan. Chill until serving time.

You may freeze the tart, but allow to come to room temperature before serving for the best flavor.

Serves 6 to 8

Almond Crust

THANKS TO THE MISSOURI EGG COUNCIL

1 cup all-purpose flour
1/3 cup sliced almonds
1/4 cup packed brown sugar
1/4 teaspoon kosher salt
6 tablespoons butter,
chilled and cubed
1/2 teaspoon almond extract
1 to 2 tablespoons (or more)
ice water

Combine the flour, almonds, brown sugar and kosher salt in a food processor. Process until the mixture resembles coarse sand. Add the butter and almond extract and process to crumbs the size of peas. Add the ice water 1 tablespoon at a time, pulsing to mix after each addition. Form into a disk on plastic wrap and chill, wrapped, for 30 minutes or longer.

Roll the dough to a 14-inch circle on a lightly floured surface. Spray a 9-inch tart pan with a removable bottom with nonstick cooking spray. Fit the pastry into the pan and trim. Freeze until firm. Bake at 425 degrees in the lower third of the oven for 20 to 25 minutes or until golden brown.

Makes 1

Grandma Eckert's
Peach Custard Pie

THANKS TO ECKERT'S COUNTRY STORE

3 eggs
1/3 cup milk
1 cup sugar
4 cups sliced peeled peaches,
   about 3 to 4 peaches
1 unbaked (9-inch) deep-dish
   pie shell

Beat the eggs in a mixing bowl. Add the milk and sugar and beat until smooth. Add the peaches and mix gently. Spoon into the pie shell. Bake at 450 degrees for 10 minutes. Reduce the oven temperature to 375 degrees and bake for 45 to 55 minutes longer or until a knife inserted into center comes out clean.

Serves 6 to 8

Praline Banana Cream Pie

2 cups chopped bananas,
   about 2 bananas
1 graham cracker pie shell
1 (1-ounce) package sugar-free
   vanilla instant pudding mix
2/3 cup nonfat dry milk powder
2 tablespoons brown
   sugar substitute
1 1/4 cups water
3/4 cup light whipped topping
1/2 cup pecans
2 tablespoons vanilla extract
1/2 cup light whipped topping

Arrange the bananas in the pie shell. Combine the pudding mix, dry milk powder and brown sugar substitute in a medium bowl. Add the water and whisk to mix well. Fold in 3/4 cup whipped topping, the pecans and vanilla. Spread evenly over the bananas. Chill for 4 hours or longer. Cut the pie into wedges to serve and top evenly with 1/2 cup whipped topping.

Serves 8

Holiday Pumpkin Cheesecake Pie

16 ounces fat-free cream cheese, softened
1 (1-ounce) package sugar-free butterscotch instant pudding mix
2/3 cup nonfat dry milk powder
1 (15-ounce) can pumpkin
1 1/2 teaspoons pumpkin pie spice
1/4 cup light whipped topping
1 graham cracker pie shell
1/2 cup light whipped topping
2 tablespoons chopped pecans

Stir the cream cheese in a large bowl until smooth. Add the pudding mix, dry milk powder, pumpkin and pumpkin pie spice; whisk until smooth. Blend in 1/4 cup whipped topping. Spread evenly in the pie shell.

Spread 1/2 cup whipped topping over the filling and sprinkle with the pecans. Chill for 2 hours or longer. Cut into eight wedges to serve.

Serves 8

Former host Dan Buck is now the Chief Executive Officer for St. Patrick's Center in St. Louis.

Strawberry Shortcake Pie

THANKS TO THE BLUE OWL RESTAURANT & BAKERY

1   (1–layer) package butter–recipe
    yellow cake mix
12 ounces cream cheese, softened
1 1/2 cups confectioners' sugar
4   ounces white chocolate, melted
1   teaspoon vanilla extract
8   ounces whipped topping
2   pints fresh strawberries, sliced
16 ounces strawberry glaze
4   ounces white chocolate
1/2 cup whipping cream
1   baked (10-inch) deep-dish
    pie shell, cooled
16 ounces whipped topping
melted white chocolate for garnish

Prepare and bake the cake mix using the package directions for one layer. Cool the cake layer and split horizontally into two layers.

Beat the cream cheese in a mixing bowl until light. Add the confectioners' sugar and beat until fluffy. Beat in 4 ounces melted white chocolate and the vanilla. Fold in 8 ounces whipped topping for the filling and frosting.

Mix the strawberries and strawberry glaze in a bowl for the strawberry glaze.

Combine 4 ounces white chocolate and the whipping cream in a saucepan. Heat until the chocolate melts, stirring to blend well for the ganache.

Spread one-third of the cream cheese filling in the pie shell. Trim the cake layers to fit the pie shell, reserving the edges. Place one cake layer cut side up in the pie shell. Spread with half the white chocolate ganache. Spread half the strawberry glaze over the ganache.

Spread the remaining white chocolate ganache on the cut side of the remaining cake layer and invert on the glaze. Frost the top and side with the remaining cream cheese filling. Top with the remaining strawberry glaze and pipe 16 ounces whipped topping around the sides.

Crumble the reserved cake trimmings and press onto the sides. Garnish with a drizzle of additional melted white chocolate.

Serves 8

Dining In

Pumpkin Yogurt Cheesecake Shake

THANKS TO THE ST. LOUIS DAIRY COUNCIL

1 (15-ounce) can pumpkin, chilled
3 ounces reduced-fat cream cheese, softened
6 ounces vanilla low-fat yogurt
2 cups low-fat milk
1/4 cup packed brown sugar
1/2 teaspoon ground cinnamon
1/8 teaspoon nutmeg
1/2 teaspoon vanilla extract
6 teaspoons graham cracker crumbs (optional)

Combine the pumpkin, cream cheese, yogurt, milk, brown sugar, cinnamon, nutmeg and vanilla in a blender and process until smooth. Pour into glasses and top with the graham cracker crumbs.

Serves 6

Our original host, Debbye Turner, is now working for the CBS morning news out of New York City.

Index

Index

Dining In

with 🦅 SHOW ME St. LOUIS

11 years of memorable recipes

To order additional copies,
visit **www.ksdk.com**

For more information, call
314-421-5055